FERENCZI FOR OUR TIME

The History of Psychoanalysis Series

Professor Brett Kahr and Professor Peter L. Rudnytsky (Series Editors)
Published and distributed by Karnac Books

Other titles in the Series

FERENCZI FOR OUR TIME

Theory and Practice

edited by
Judit Szekacs-Weisz
and Tom Keve

Routledge
Taylor & Francis Group

LONDON AND NEW YORK

First published 2012 by
Karnac Books Ltd.

Published 2018 by Routledge
2 Park Square, Milton Park, Abingdon, Oxon OX14 4RN
711 Third Avenue, New York, NY 10017, USA

Routledge is an imprint of the Taylor & Francis Group, an informa business

British Library Cataloguing in Publication Data

A C.I.P. for this book is available from the British Library

ISBN 9781780490403 (pbk)

Edited, designed and produced by The Studio Publishing Services Ltd
www.publishingservicesuk.co.uk
e-mail: studio@publishingservicesuk.co.uk

CONTENTS

ACKNOWLEDGEMENTS

It is a pleasure to thank all the authors for their excellent and insightful contributions and for their patience through the several years that it has taken to refine this volume. The continued support and helpful, critical comments of Professor Ferenc Erős is gratefully acknowledged. Mrs Anna Kovács aided us with research and careful copy-editing. The professional and personal support of Kathleen Kelley-Lainé over the years is also greatly valued and much appreciated by both of us.

We are particularly indebted to Dr Judith Dupont for all her support over the years and her generous permission to allow us to make use of original documents and previously unpublished images from the Ferenczi Archives.

We thank Mr Ivan Ward for his good-natured support over the years and for the facilities of the Freud Museum, of which we availed ourselves. Thanks are also due to Ken Robinson and the Archives of the British Psychoanalytical Society and Institute of Psychoanalysis for access and permission to reproduce correspondence (and photographs). We are happy to thank Her Excellency, Mrs Katalin Bogyay, Hungary's ambassador to UNESCO for continued interest in, and support of, our projects and for her belief that social sciences and psychoanalytic ideas are a valuable part of a nation's culture.

Last but certainly not least, we are very pleased to acknowledge helpful advice of our Series Editors, Professors Peter Rudnytsky and Brett Kahr and are grateful to them and to Mr Oliver Rathbone of Karnac Books for inclusion in their History of Psychoanalysis series.

Judit Szekacs-Weisz and Tom Keve
Imago International, London, April 2012

Editors' note

During the compilation of this volume, we faced, yet again the issue of multiple and confused use of Hungarian names. This is not just an editorial issue, but is an important reflection of diverse aspects of persecution and emigration. We feel the best we can do now to help clarification is to give a bilingual list of some of the most frequently occurring names,

English usage	Hungarian original
Alice Balint	Bálint-Székely-Kovács Alíz
Michael Balint	Bálint Mihály
Ivan Fonagy	Fónagy Iván
Anton von Freund	tószegi Freund Antal
Istvan Hollos	Hollós István
Vilma Kovacs	Kovács Vilma
Frederic Kovacs	Kovács Frigyes
Edith Ludowyk-Gyomroi	Ludowyk-Gyömrői Edit
Sandor Rado	Radó Sándor
Geza Roheim	Róheim Géza
Istvan Szekacs-Schonberger	Székács-Schönberger István
Judit Szekacs-Weisz	Székács Judit

Judith Dupont née Dormandi, the granddaughter of Vilma Kovács and niece of Alice Balint, was born in 1925 in Budapest. Her mother, Olga Székely-Kovács, was a painter and sculptor who portrayed numerous psychoanalysts. Her father, László Dormandi, was the owner of the Hungarian publishing house Pantheon and the author of several novels. She grew up in the house of her grandparents, Vilma and Frigyes Kovács, in Budapest. The psychoanalytic polyclinic was located in this building (Meszaros street 12) and it was also the home of the Balint family. In 1938, the Dormandis emigrated to Paris, where Judith studied medicine and trained as a psychoanalyst after the end of the war. In 1954 she became a member of the Association Psychanalytique de France. She worked as a child analyst in different institutions and also in private practice where she treated adult patients. In 1969, she founded the journal *Le Coq-Héron*. One of the journal's main themes is the history of psychoanalysis, with special emphasis on Hungarian psychoanalysis. Dr Dupont has been a major force in the publication and republication of works by Sandor Ferenczi and Michael and Alice Balint. She has also been the keeper of the Ferenczi Archives and guardian of Ferenczi's heritage world wide.

Ferenc Erős studied psychology and literature at the ELTE University in Budapest, and graduated in 1969. He obtained his PhD in 1986, and has been Doctor of the Hungarian Academy of Sciences (DSc) since 2002. Currently, he is Professor of Social Psychology at the University of Pécs, where he has directed a doctoral programme in psychoanalytic studies since 1997. Simultaneously, he directs a social psychological research unit at the Research Institute of Psychology of the Hungarian Academy of Sciences in Budapest. In the academic year 2010–2011, he was senior fellow at the Collegium Budapest, Institute for Advanced Studies. The focus of his present research includes the social and cultural history of psychoanalysis in central Europe, psychoanalytic theory, and cultural memory. He edited the Hungarian translation of the Freud–Ferenczi correspondence, and he published— in collaboration with Judit Szekacs—the correspondence between Sandor Ferenczi and Ernest Jones. He is author of several scientific books and articles in his areas of research.

Gábor Flaskay is a training analyst of the Hungarian Psychoanalytical Society. He belongs to the second post-war generation of psychoanalysts in Budapest and is a leading figure in the scientific and organisational life of the Society. István Székács-Schonberger, a disciple of Michael Balint, and the theory of object relations were major influences on his analytic thinking. His book, *Analytical Psychotherapy in Practice*, was published in 2010 by Medicina, Budapest.

György Hidas, psychiatrist and training analyst, is one of the central figures of the renewal of post-war psychoanalysis in Hungary and the re-creation of the Hungarian Psychoanalytical Society. Founder member and President of the Sándor Ferenczi Society (1988–1998), he is the author of a wide scope of more than seventy publications ranging from the history of psychoanalysis (with a special focus on Sandor Ferenczi's life and work, his trauma theory, and place and role in the international movement of his time) to more general clinical and technical issues. Lately, he developed a method for working through aspects of the prenatal relationship in the mother–baby dyad. He remains a most respected teacher and therapist of different generations.

Jennifer Johns is a Fellow of the British Psychoanalytical Society. From a psychoanalytic family, she became a GP before training as an analyst. She was influenced by reading the work of Michael and Enid Balint with general practitioners and chose Enid Balint as her training analyst. She also received some supervision from Donald Winnicott, among others. Dr Johns has always remained interested in psycho-somatic medicine, particularly relating to eye problems. She has an interest in teaching, both fellow professionals and students, about psychoanalysis. In addition to her private practice in psychoanalysis, she has worked in the Department of Psychotherapy at University College hospital in London, and has been Chair of the Winnicott Trust.

Kathleen Kelley-Lainé was born in Budapest, emigrated to Canada as a child, grew up in Toronto, and has been living in France for more than thirty-five years. She is a psychoanalyst in private practice, works in three languages (English, French, and Hungarian). She is a member of the Société Psychoanalytic de Paris, of the International Psychoanalytic Association, and an honorary member of the Hungarian Psycho-analytic Society, as well as the Sándor Ferenczi Society, Budapest. Pub-lications include *Peter Pan ou l'Enfant Triste* (1992); *Peter Pan, the Story of Lost Childhood* (1995); *Pan Peter avagy a Szomoru Gyerek* (1996); *Contes Cruels de La Mondilasation* with Dominique Rousset (2001); *A globaliza-cio kegyetlen meséi -A világ a díványon* with Dominique Rousset (2003).

Tom Keve studied physics at Manchester University, has a PhD in Crystallography from Imperial College, London, and is a Fellow of the Institute of Physics. Since retiring from an active career in scientific research and industry, he has become an author, with a special inter-est in the history of science and the history of psychoanalysis. His book, *Triad: The Physicists, The Analysts, The Kabbalists* (in its French translation, *Trois explications du monde*) was shortlisted for the 2010 European Book Prize. Together with Judit Szekacs-Weisz, he co-edited *Ferenczi and his World*, published by Karnac Books, London in 2012. Dr Keve is co-founder and secretary of Imago International.

Meira Likierman is a consultant child and adolescent psychothera-pist. She has for many years taught on Melanie Klein and led the doctoral programme at the Child and Family Department of the Tavistock Clinic in London. She lectures in the UK, Europe, and the USA. Her book, *Melanie Klein: Her Work in Context*, was published in 2001 by Continuum.

Joan Raphael-Leff, Fellow of the British Psychoanalytical Society and Member of the Independent Group, leads the UCL/Anna Freud Centre Academic Faculty for Psychoanalytic Research. Previously she was Professor of Psychoanalysis at the Centre for Psychoanalytic Studies, University of Essex, and Head of University College London's MSc in Psychoanalytic Developmental Psychology. In her clinical training Professor Raphael-Leff was supervised by Enid Balint and Paula Heimann. In 1998 she founded COWAP, the International Psychoanalytic Association's Committee on Women. Over the past 40 years she has specialised in emotional aspects of Reproduction and early Parenting, authoring over 100 publications and eleven books, including: *Psychological Processes of Childbearing; Pregnancy—The Inside Story; Parent–Infant Psychodynamics: Wild Things, Mirrors and Ghosts; Spilt Milk: Perinatal Loss and Breakdown; Ethics of Psychoanalysis; Between Sessions and Beyond the Couch; Female Experience: Four Generations of British Women Psychoanalysts on Work with Women* (co-edited with R. J. Perelberg) and most recently *The Anna Freud Tradition: Lines of Development; Evolution of Theory and Practice over the Decades* (co-edited with N. T. Malberg) and *Working with Teenage Parents*. She lectures in the UK and abroad, and teaches primary health workers on six continents.

Catherine Reverzy was a psychiatrist and psychoanalyst born in Paris of a Swiss father and French mother. She studied medicine in Lausanne and presented her thesis on Sandor Ferenczi. Ferenczi's and Michael Balint's clinical and theoretical works had a formative effect on her professional development and, later on, her writing. The first of her three major books *Couloir de Nuit* (1982) was an autobiographical study of living with mental illness in the family, while *Femme d'Aventure*, penetrates the psychic world of women engaged in extreme risk taking. Her interest in the role of the body in psychiatric treatment resulted in her training in different methods of relaxation. On "Thalassa and regression" she wrote, "The desire to return to oneself, even if it means a detour via the 'great all' is on the side of the 'life instinct'. This does not mean that our vitality cannot end up in an accident or death if we commit a fatal error or if our luck runs out . . . In that case, we find ourselves on the road of 'eternal life' . . ." On 15 April 2008, after a long illness, Catherine embarked on the great adventure of death.

Ágnes Riskó is a clinical psychologist and training analyst of the Hungarian Psychoanalytical Society. After working with psychiatric patients on a psychiatric ward ("Maison jaune"), in 1990 she moved to the National Institute of Oncology in Budapest and began field-work with cancer inpatients. As a regular team member on the oncological ward, she has numerous opportunities for observation on a daily basis utilising projective tests (Rorschach, Szondi), counselling, practising psychoanalytical psychotherapy with patients and their relatives. During the first ten years of her oncological work, she undertook a so-called "intensive supervison" led by her psycho-analyst, István Székács-Schönberger (two sessions weekly, on the couch). Together, they worked out certain parts of psychoanalytical oncopsychology. Now Riskó continues this process with her young colleagues at the Hungarian Psychoanalytical Society. Recently, she has turned her interest to exploring the spontaneous artwork created by cancer patients during chemotherapy.

Rachel Rosenblum, psychiatrist and psychoanalyst, is a member of the Paris Psychoanalytic Society, where her seminar on "Trauma survivors and the dangers of bearing witness" has explored since 1998 the survival strategies elaborated by the survivors of major traumas. On what conditions can such strategies be successful? When do they end up in tragedy? These are the questions she adresses in a series of papers including: "Peut-on Mourir de dire? Sarah Kofman & Primo Levi"; "Presenting the past: psychoanalysis and the sociology of mis-remembering"; "Un destin écran ou l'homme qui avait deux des-tines", all in *Revue Française de Psychanalyse*; "Postponing trauma: the dangers of telling", in *International Journal of Psychoanalysis*; and "Shoah and psychoanalysis", in *Psychoanalysis International*.

Jonathan Sklar is a training analyst and Fellow of the British Psycho-analytic Society. His book, *Landscapes of the Dark: History, Trauma, Psychoanalysis* was published by Karnac in September 2011. Dr Sklar works in private analytic practice in London.

Harold Stewart, a trusted and respected personification of the inde-pendent spirit of British psychoanalysis, brought original thinking and commonsense humanity to the practice of his profession. Born in London, trained at UCL and UCSH, in 1947, a year after qualifying in medicine, he entered the National Health Service (NHS) at its inception. He was drawn first towards hypnotherapy, then to psychoanalysis, as a more sensitive, productive, and far-reaching method of exploring and understanding patients' experience. He was consultant psychiatrist at the Paddington Centre for Psychotherapy and consultant psychotherapist at the Tavistock Clinic until his retirement in 1989. His many publications include two books, *Psychic Experience and Problems of Technique* (1992), and *Michael Balint, Object Relations Pure and Applied* (1996). Dr Stewart died on 25 June 2005. His contribution to the present volume was one of his last publications.

Judit Szekacs-Weisz is a bilingual psychoanalyst and psychotherapist, a member of the British Psychoanalytical Society, the Group of Independent Psychoanalysts, and training analyst of the Hungarian Psychoanalytical Society. Born and educated (mostly) in Budapest, she has absorbed the ideas and way of thinking of Ferenczi, the Balints, Hermann, and Rajka as an integral part of a "professional mother tongue". The experience of living and working in a totalitarian regime sensitised her to the social and individual aspects of trauma, identity formation, and strategies of survival. Dr Szekacs-Weisz was a founding member of the Sándor Ferenczi Society, Budapest. In 1990, she moved to London, where, with a small group of psychoanalysts, therapists, artists, and social scientists, she founded Imago East West, and later the Multilingual Psychotherapy Centre (MLPC), to create a space where diverse experiences of living and changing context and language in different cultures can be explored and creative solutions found. She is the author of several articles and co-editor of *Lost Childhood and the Language of Exile* (Freud Museum & Imago East West, 2004). Together with Tom Keve, she co-edited *Ferenczi and his World*, published by Karnac, London in 2012. Dr Szekacs-Weisz is President of Imago International.

Margaret Tonnesmann is a member of the British Psychoanalytical Society especially esteemed for her scholarship in relation to the writings of Freud and Winnicott. At the Institute of Psychoanalysis in London, she taught the Freud seminars for many years and also led seminars of Winnicott's work. Her teaching extended to such institutions as the Tavistock Clinic, the British Association of Psychotherapists and to University College London, as well as many teaching assignments abroad in Europe.

Peter L. Rudnytsky

"Introductions should be enticements". I cannot do better than to reprise the words of Joan Raphael-Leff in her own insightful and erudite prolegomenon to this splendid volume.

A companion to *Ferenczi and His World*, and simultaneously the realisation of the editors' dream of bringing forth in its totality their "London Ferenczi Reader", *Ferenczi for Our Time* stakes its greatest claim on the reader's attention by making manifest the contours of a distinctively Ferenczian tradition in the history of psychoanalysis. In so doing, the essays gathered here take us on an intellectual journey from the pre-First World War period in which Melanie Klein first arrived in Budapest to our twenty-first-century moment, symbolised by the curving image of Chicago refracted in Anish Kapoor's sculpture, *Cloud Gate*, also known as "The Bean", that adorns the cover.

After the keynote struck by Joan Raphael-Leff, who justly highlights "the radicality of Ferenczi's perspective" and his fecundity as "the ancestor of many theoretical innovators" who propagated his "object-relations interpersonal ethos", noting in this connection the divergent conceptions of the baby espoused by Freud and Ferenczi, our journey begins with the contributions by Gábor Flaskay and Meira Likierman on Ferenczi and Klein. Flaskay calls attention to the widespread underestimation of Ferenczi's influence on Klein, a phenomenon at least in part explained by Likierman's observation that Ferenczi's "more personal elements were absorbed by Klein in unconscious, and not only in conscious, ways". Both authors under-score Ferenczi's early attention to transference interpretation, which leads Likierman to speak of "a theory of technique passed from Ferenczi via Klein into contemporary thinking", most notably in the work of Betty Joseph, according to which it is "specifically internal objects that were transferred on to the arena of analysis, and not so much people from the patient's past".

If seeing Klein in Ferenczi's image takes some of Ferenczi's own vaunted "elasticity", it requires no such stretch of the imagination to follow Margaret Tonnesmann in moving from Ferenczi to Winnicott. Like Likierman, Tonnesmann chooses as her point of departure Ferenczi's 1913 paper, "Stages in the development of the sense of real-ity", and proceeds to mount a nuanced argument that, despite his attention to ego development in infancy, Ferenczi's was originally a "one-body psychology"; only during the 1920s did his theoretical orientation shift to a "two-body psychology", such as was later elab-orated by Winnicott. Tonnesmann sees the greatest affinity between these two masters in their concern with "pathogenic early traumata", as well as in their shared conviction that "privation and de-privation, to use Winnicott's terminology, lead to narcissistic splits of the self and only by re-experiencing such early traumata during analysis can these splits be healed".

Tonnesmann closes with some reflections on Françoise Dolto, the *grande dame* of French psychoanalysis, whose connections to Ferenczi are in turn much more fully explored by Kathleen Kelley-Lainé. Playing off Ferenczi's bioanalytic speculations in *Thalassa* against Dolto's use of the metaphor of the wave and the ocean to convey her distinctive understanding of the interplay between the life and death instincts, Kelley-Lainé explains how "the concept of 'symbolic castra-tion' is a fundamental principle of psychic growth" for Dolto. On a personal level, moreover, both Ferenczi and Dolto were "highly appreciated for their innovative and creative contributions to psycho-analysis, while at the same time [they] were ultimately marginalised for those very reasons". Kelley-Lainé compares Ferenczi's relationship to Freud to Dolto's equally close, yet ultimately tragic, relationship to Lacan: "Both separated from their mentors for ethical reasons; both felt that their mentors had deviated from their own symbolic values".

The longest section of this book is fittingly centred on Michael Balint, who forms the most direct link between Ferenczi and modern British psychoanalysis. Harold Stewart provides an overview of Balint's own contributions, singling out the distinction between benign and malignant regression as his most important concept, while Judith Dupont introduces us to his first wife, Alice, and Jennifer Johns provides a loving and detailed tribute to his third wife, Enid, who was Johns' training analyst. Both of these extraordinary women collaborated so deeply with Michael Balint in his creative work that, as he wrote of Alice after her premature death in 1939, "often it was just chance that decided which of us should publish a particular idea". As Johns recounts, Enid Balint warned against the dangers of "understanding too quickly" what is being communicated by a patient, while at the same time cautioning against any abdication of "the strictly analytic technique of listening for associations for the more 'kindly' one of friendliness and warmth, which could leave the ill, needy part of the patient unrecognised and abandoned". This pivotal section on the Balints is rounded out by György Hidas's reminiscences of Mészáros Street 12, the Budapest residence which was owned by Alice Balint's mother, Vilma Kovács, before becoming the site of the Psychoanalytic Clinic, directed first by Ferenczi himself and then by Michael Balint, as well as by Catherine Reverzy's intriguing deployment of Balint's antithesis between the character types of the *ocnophile* and the *philobat* to illuminate the feat of Sir Edmund Hillary, who, in 1953, together with his Nepalese Sherpa, Tensing Norgay, became the first climbers to have scaled Mount Everest.

The final two sections expand the scope of the book both conceptually and clinically. The theme of traumatic legacies conjoins the chapters of co-editor Judit Szekacs-Weisz and Rachel Rosenblum. Szekacs-Weisz draws not only on her expertise in treating members of the "post-war 'second generation'" in her native Hungary, but also on her own experience as a "child of the Iron Curtain", to elucidate the strategies that have made Hungarians into "professional survivors". Rosenblum, for her part, tells the shattering story of Sarah Kofman, the brilliant French philosopher who—like a litany of others who dared to speak of the unspeakable—ended her life in suicide. Rosenblum offers compelling readings of Kofman's commentaries on Freud, Kafka, Hitchcock, and others as *heterobiographies*, which Rosenblum defines as "speaking of others as an indirect way of speaking about oneself", before turning to Kofman's autobiography, *Rue Ordener, rue Labat*, the "unbearable text" that was "the raw exposure of the distress of a little girl torn between two mothers"—one Jewish, the other Christian, both of whom she eventually betrayed"—while her father was lost, rounded up, deported, and assassinated at Auschwitz". Suffice it to say that the spirit of Ferenczi, both as a theorist and as himself a victim of trauma, is never far from these haunting pages.

The final section rings changes on the theme of "revolts of the body". Jonathan Sklar offers a series of clinical vignettes in support of his "plea to take the body of the patient as seriously as the mind and language". Ágnes Riskó reports on her work as an analyst in Budapest with both inpatients and outpatients suffering from malignant lymphomas. Following Balint, Riskó sees cancer as representing "the basic fault and the fearful inner 'bad,' which attacks and fills the diseased person from the inside with oral aggressiveness". She likewise echoes Winnicott in saying, "there is no such thing as a patient", but, rather, only a patient and his or her family, along with the health-care team involved in the treatment. Over the years, Riskó has increasingly found herself trying to help her colleagues and the patient's relatives as well as the cancer-stricken patient.

The phrase "revolt of the body" is taken from the erudite essay by Ferenc Erős that brings this volume to a close. Erős's primary concern, however, is with another phrase, "poor Konrad", used by the hero of the novel *Imago*, published in 1906 by the Swiss–German writer Carl Spitteler, to refer to his own body. The latter locution found its way into Freud's correspondence with both Ferenczi and Jung, and thereby became part of the psychoanalytic vernacular, while Spitteler's title was appropriated six years later by Hanns Sachs as the name for the first journal dedicated to psychoanalysis and the human sciences. As Erős points out, "poor Konrad" was originally the moniker of an alliance that, in 1514, "launched an uprising in Württemberg" and, in so doing, formed "an antecedent to the great German peasant wars in Luther's age". "Poor Konrad," in Erős's incisive exposition, thus becomes a nexus not simply between psychoanalysis and literature but, no less profoundly, between psychoanalysis and politics.

Glancing back at the previous volume, Judit Szekacs-Weisz notes in her Preface that a *leitmotif* of *Ferenczi and His World* was that the discipline of psychoanalysis was collectively "created by an expanding circle of thinkers and practitioners who not only practised but 'lived'" this new form of personal and professional identity. If psycho-analysis is to prosper in the twenty-first century, it will only be because we continue to live and breathe it for ourselves. That an increasing number of present-day thinkers and practitioners have found no greater source of inspiration than Sandor Ferenczi is proof enough that he is, indeed, an analyst for our time.

Judit Szekacs-Weisz

In our first volume, *Ferenczi and His World*, we tried to conjure up the image, personality, innovations (both theoretical and technical), and teachings of Sandor Ferenczi, the legendary—and for some decades, spectacularly forgotten—figure of the international psychoanalytical movement. All his life he worked from Budapest, at the time the "second capital" of psychoanalysis. Always sensitive to overt and undercurrent processes in science, society, and culture, he was a highly respected and influential figure. A doctor of the mind to whom colleagues from all over the world could refer the most difficult cases, he became an eminent and passionate propagator of the new science: psychoanalysis.

"He made all analysts his students", wrote Freud in his obituary in 1933 and, indeed, the list of names most closely related to Ferenczi and the Budapest School is very substantial. Let us mention a few of them: Ernest Jones, Melanie Klein, Sándor Rado, Géza Róheim, John Rickman, Clara Thomson, Georg Groddeck, Therese Benedek, Margaret Mahler, Franz Alexander, Eugenie Sokolnicka, Rene Spitz, Otto Rank István Holls, the Balints (of course), Vilma Kovács, Antal tószeghi Freund, Imre Hermann, Iván Fónagy, Edith Ludowyk-Gyömrői. His analysands (a term also coined by Ferenczi) and students carried his ideas along with them well beyond the borders of Hungary.

The first volume of our collected papers devoted to "Rekindling the Spirit of the Budapest School", was a testimony to the extraordinary professional and human relationship that formed between Ferenczi and other leading figures in the early history of psychoanalysis. An obvious message of the previous volume was that psychoanalysis has been created by an expanding circle of thinkers and practitioners who not only practised but also "lived" psychoanalysis. Without understanding the true nature of their ideas and controversies, without acknowledging and integrating the fundamental contributions they made, the picture of our professional past would be found fragmented and wanting.

Soon after Ferenczi's death, the development and continuity of the movement was forcefully interrupted: history interfered. Making sense of what happened—the overwhelming effects of persecution, successful and failed emigration, loss of lives, homes, and language—was to become a major part of our work, both in our consulting rooms and our private lives.

Ferenczi for Our Time presents contributions from British, French, American, and Hungarian analysts of the second, third, and even fourth generation, who deal with different dimensions of experiencing the external and internal world. These papers explore linkages between Ferenczi and the works of Winnicott, Klein, Alice, Michael, and Enid Balint, the British Independents, as well as French analytical thought related to Dolto and beyond.

The reader will also become acquainted with original documents of a revived Hungarian psychoanalytical world and new voices of Budapest. "The Balints" chapter invites the reader to listen to colleagues sharing memories, recollections, and images—allowing a personal glimpse into the life and professional–human environment of these extraordinary personalities.

The topics discussed here are wide ranging: possibilities and impossibilities of elaborating social and individual traumata, child analysis and development, body and mind, and clinical aspects of working with psychosomatic diseases. Functions and dysfunctions of societal and individual memory are explored as signifying "blinded" spots in our vision of external and psychic reality, as well as the vicissitudes of generational transmission of trauma. The scope of these papers covers methodology, theory, and clinical practice.

As we emphasised in *Ferenczi and his World*, our contributors have all been inspired by conferences and workshops organised in London during the past fifteen years. We also said that by reviving images of a slightly forgotten past, we aim not only to rekindle the spirit of the Budapest School and of Sandor Ferenczi, but also hope to create a thinking space for the reader: a space where questioning, reflection, and understanding can take place and where associations to our own experiences related to "our time" can be made.

Intimacy and trauma

Joan Raphael-Leff

". . . don't read the introduction," warned someone recommending a novel, "it gives everything away."

Introductions should be enticements—an invitation to partake. In introducing this book, I hope to whet your interest without pre-empting your sense of discovery. Suffice to say that the many chapters herein celebrate one of the most innovative and impassioned of all psychoanalysts, whose work anticipated many of today's findings: in psychosomatics, neonatal research, neuropsychology, physics, pedagogy, and attachment theory. In this context, the present volume marks the contemporary renaissance of engagement with his ideas.

Psychoanalytically, Sandor Ferenczi's thinking inspired inter-per- sonal, intersubjective, and relational theories. However, his work cannot be understood outside of its gestational influences. Central among these is his sparring partner Freud and the designation as "crown prince". Our view of the murky depths of this "harmonious father–son" collaboration (as Ferenczi (1932) himself referred to it in his *Clinical Diary*, p. 185) tends to be overshadowed by Ferenczi's fall from grace in his last years, increasingly isolated by the fraternal primal horde's jealousy and hostility. However, the profundity of his filial link is evident in the emotional timbre of the published thou- sand-plus letters between Freud and Ferenczi—an ambivalently

Sandor Ferenczi, by Olga Székely-Kovács.

charged correspondence that spans the twenty-five years of their turbulent relationship. The Freud–Ferenczi friendship was also punctuated by joint projects, numerous exchange visits, and holidays together throughout Europe, as well as a trip to the USA.

However, their journey to London in 1912 was cancelled as both men rushed back to Vienna from Italy, when Freud's daughter Mathilde fell ill (Falzeder, 2002, p. 163, n1). Over the previous four years, Freud had harboured a cherished wish that Sandor would marry Mathilde, while he, in turn, was engaged in agonised deliberations about whether to passively surrender to the "maternal subjugation" of family friend Gizella, or succumb to the "dangerous attractiveness" of her twenty-four-year-old daughter Elma, his analysand . . . Eventually, nineteen years after the beginning of their relationship, Ferenczi did marry Gizella, but their wedding ceremony was marred by news that her former husband died of a heart attack that day, aggravating Ferenczi's guilt about "taking the mother away from the father".

Ferenczi, accompanied by Gizella, did make it to London fifteen years later, on their way back from his 1927 lecture series in New York. He gave a lecture on "the adaptation of the family to the child" to the British Psychological Society. Ferenczi also returned to England in 1929, when he gave the presidential address to the International Psycho-Analytical Congress in Oxford. On this occasion, he drew attention to the importance of the menstruation complex, and placed it as being of equal importance with the castration complex.

Their bi-directional "intimate community of life, feeling, and interest" (as Freud summed it up on 11 January 1933, just a few months before Sandor's death (Falzeder, 2000, p. 446)) was particularly pertinent to this eighth of twelve children, resonating with the tenderness he craved from his strict unbending mother and grief for the premature loss of his kind father, who favoured him.

Themes of loss, lust, and lies reverberate throughout their intense relationship, reiterated time and again over the years, seemingly both to safeguard and repair the bond (". . . it is necessary to write about the same old things / In the same way, repeating the same things over and over / For love to continue and be gradually different", John Ashbery says in *Late Echo* (1979, p. 164)). And indeed, regression, emotional repetition, authenticity, and, indeed, love become the hallmark of Ferenczi's professional technique.

Ferenczi's "burning desire" to win Freud's *paternal* approval (Ferenczi, 1932, p. 185) renders his early psychoanalytical writings an extension and clinical elaboration of the ideas of his "Dear Professor". But this complex relationship was also permeated by more feminine feelings: ". . . the transference will certainly 'fecundate' me", Ferenczi writes on 10 July 1916 (Falzeder & Brabant, 1996, p. 132) after the second brief period of analysis. And the oceanic reference in "[T]he affects unleashed by the treatment have been undulating up and down in me" (Falzeder & Brabant, 1996, p. 150, 30 Oct 1916) echoes desire for mutual merger and a thalassic regressive yearning to be re-immersed in the *maternal* intrauterine sea, metaphorically located within.

To Freud, transference manifests in the acting out of unconscious phantasies as a defence against remembering. The silencing effects of the unresolved transference are apparent in Ferenczi's inability to fully find his own voice in his first and further psychoanalytic writings, an inhibition he later ascribed to Freud's too muchness.

On 6 October 1910, long before the analysis began, Freud had professed, "I am also not that ψα superman whom we have constructed, and I also haven't overcome the countertransference" (Falzeder & Brabant, 1996, p. 221). In 1921, Ferenczi confided to his new friend Groddeck: "I could never be completely free and open with him . . . he was too big for me, there was too much of the father" (Fortune, 2002). Nine years later, Ferenczi accosted Freud with not having perceived the negative transference, adding, "I do not . . . share your view that the process of healing is an unimportant procedure, or one that should be neglected, which one ought to neglect only because it doesn't appear to us to be so interesting" (Falzeder & Brabant, 2000, p. 383), to which Freud responded affectionately three days later, writing,

> Whereby you fail to consider that this analysis goes back fifteen years, and that at the time we were by no means so sure that these reactions could be expected in every case. At least, I wasn't. You yourself [should] consider how long this analysis would have had to last until the inimical impulses in our excellent relationship had succeeded in getting through. (Falzeder & Brabant, p. 383)

Despite accolades from his British editor, John Rickman, Ferenczi often plays down his own originality, appeasingly depicting "active" techniques as "adjuvants in reinforcing the Freudian method" (Ferenczi, 1926, p. 8). He might have felt constrained by criticism and probably the pledge to fellow members of Freud's "Secret Committee"[1] in 1912, after Adler and Stekel defected and as Jung prepared to jump ship, that none would make any public departures from the "fundamental tenets" of psychoanalytic theory before discussing this with the others. Increasingly treated by these colleagues with "a mixture of admiration and guarded suspicion" (Balint, 1933, p. 216), Ferenczi trod a narrow path of "manifest belief and latent disbelief in the father" (Falzeder & Brabant, 1996, p. 109).

Nevertheless, as Ferenczi urges us in his *Clinical Diary*, that "the map should never be confused with the territory" (Ferenczi, 1932, p. 144). The loyalty of his disciples and their worldwide influence proves Clara Thompson's point that, although conformist in his writing (in her view "more Freudian than Freud" (Thompson, 1988, p. 185)), Ferenczi's *thinking* deviated quite radically from that outlined in much of his early psychoanalytic publications. The full extent of his professional originality was accessible to students, with whom he felt able to express his own ideas, and who, in turn, recognised the importance of his innovations. Furthermore, as the contributions to this volume attest, when released, Ferenczi's soaring imagination has the capacity to inspire others, evoking a whimsicality in those around him, resonating in bold ideas and "quixotic" phrasing.

In treating Ferenczi as the *enfant terrible* of psychoanalysis, we tend to overlook his eminent pre-analytic career in neurology. Before meeting Freud, he had already written some fifty papers. Intimations of the independence of mind of his late work feature in throw-away lines and topics, such as his 1899 work on telepathy and spiritism (an interest later shared with Freud) and hypnotism; his 1901 paper on "Love and science"; his insistence (in 1902) that transvestites be granted public outage; his demands in 1905 for healthier social conditions for the disadvantaged, for prostitutes, and decriminalisation of homosexuality; or the 1908 rider that over-stimulation of babies is just as disastrous as neglect. Similarly pioneering are his early psychoanalytic explorations of the power dynamics in the consulting room; his attention to time; to grafitti; to foreplay; the intersubjective perspective on pre-Oedipal development and separation; allusions to primal love and familial transmission of trauma; elaboration of the stages in the development of a sense of reality and of the disproportionate mismatch between infantile needs and unconscious parental expectations, etc. Originality overrode submission as concepts such as introjection; amphimyxis; overcompensatory symmetrical touching; presymbolic corporeality; intermeshing mother–son "dialogues of the unconscious" and his unique understanding of unconscious transgenerational transmissions, all crept into his writing, possibly due to enthusiastic unawareness of just how perturbing the nature of his intense curiosity and experimentation were within the institutionalised psychoanalytic "confusion of tongues", as Balint, Gedo, Rachman, and others suggest.

It is difficult to convey the radicality of Ferenczi's perspective, zooming from the prevailing focus on the Oedipal within an intrapsychic psychology to the *pre-Oedipal, intersubjective and real*. He had a unique view of the primary interactive dyad separating out of an archaic mother–baby "mesh" and the potential mismatch between the exquisitely sensitive infant's craving for responsive tenderness and the misattuned parent's libidinal desires. Ferenczi was the ancestor of many theoretical innovators for whom the relationship between self and internalised object representations is the core. Analysands and followers shared his dynamic perspective, and, once dispersed, they disseminated this object-relations interpersonal ethos around the world. Among these were Franz Alexander, Alice and Michael Balint, Therese Benedek, Izette de Forest, Georg Groddeck, Erich Fromm, Frieda Fromm-Reichmann, Imre Hermann, István Hollós, Karen Horney, Ignotus,[2] Ernest Jones, Melanie Klein, Barbara Lantos, Alice Lowell, Margaret Mahler, John Rickman, Géza Róheim, and Clara von Thompson, all of whom benefited from his warm intuitive understanding and capacity to couple curiosity, playfulness, and experimentation with self-critical evaluation.

At the bedrock of all psychoanalytic theorising lies a baby. The particular infant each theoretician holds in mind reflects developmental dynamics. This then dictates corresponding requisite parenting. In other words, theory-generating internal working models composed of mental representations of infantile endowment and growth are coupled with commensurate care. Such conceptualisation also indicates the theoretician's beliefs about the aetiology of psychopathology, and, hence, appropriate treatment (Raphael-Leff, 1986). Ferenczi's innovation is to link the two. By analogy, process and outcome goals of the analytic relationship come to mirror good parenting.

Civilised by paternal law, Freud's baby emerged solipsistically out of primary narcissism within an anaclitic attachment. By contrast, Ferenczi's primarily loving but vulnerable baby was deemed actively object seeking from the start, requiring empathic maternal responsiveness, and subject to precocious wisdom, but also dissociation due to inexplicable parental passions and hypocrisy.

The distinction is profound. Freudian conceptualisation of a gradually cohering fragmented and non-differentiated ego contrasts markedly with the idea of a pristine whole and undivided innate ego, as postulated by Ferenczi (and, later, British Object Relations theorists, Ferenczi-influenced Balint and Klein, as well as Fairbairn and Guntrip). As I have elaborated elsewhere (Raphael-Leff, 2012), this distinction underpins fundamentally discrepant views of babies: as *a simpler form of life which will ultimately evolve* into the complexity and autonomy of adulthood, as opposed to *an innately complex neonate whose intense interior life will diminish over time* (after what Ferenczi–Alexander deemed the "great intimidation".

Today's neonatal research dates spontaneous alert engagement even earlier, confirming the active newborn's need for reciprocally receptive companionship. Sophisticated microanalysis captures the complex bi-directional interactional patterns between carers and infants (Beebe & Lachman, 2002; Gerhardt, 2004). Studies show that some innate characteristics, such as sociability, imagination, and curiosity, flourish in young children but might deteriorate through lack of stimulation, educational inhibition, or emotional pressure (Gerhardt, 2004). Similarly, psychoneurology reveals long-lasting synaptical damage in the brain due to chronic misperception, childhood neglect, as well as the dissociative processes and repressions of post traumatic stress disorder (PTSD) (Balbernie, 2001).

Lacking such sophisticated research techniques, Ferenczi drew on his own bodily reservoir of sensually registered emotions in observing and theorising about the infant's presymbolic experience and its enigmatic bodily eruptions in adulthood. Not only has his pioneering work on psychosomatic processes and their bypassing of thought burgeoned beyond his own wildest dreams, but neuro-psycho-analytical research has confirmed the persistence of sub-cortically implanted non-declarative memories of implicit and procedural bodily experience (Bucci, 2002; Schore, 2001).

Working with severely damaged borderline and regressed adult patients, it was Ferenczi who first linked early nurture and psycho-analytic treatment, identifying the risk of the therapist duplicating the "pathogenic trauma" of parental failures through mal-attunement or hypocritical insincerity. On the basis of his own analysis ("finished, but not terminated"), as well as those he conducted, his latter-day perspective provided better understanding of parental weaknesses, and, by analogy, ways in which the personal attributes and foibles of each analyst–patient couple have an impact on each other. Inevitably, awareness of unconscious dialogical forces in the consulting room led Ferenczi to consider *countertransference as an essential part of therapy*— a phenomenon which, in his day, was regarded as a disturbing by-product of psychoanalysis.

Much later, following Heimann's 1950 paper, countertransference became central to the British debate between Independents and Kleinians, and, later still, was a crucial issue for those interrogating the "new orthodoxy" of ego psychology in the USA in the 1970s. Notably, the proponents, Merton Gill, Roy Schafer, and George Klein, were affiliated to the Budapest school via their Hungarian-born mentor, psychologist David Rapaport. Thus, indirectly, they shared Ferenczi as a common "ancestor" with the British Independent Group. They challenged the monolithic paradigm of their day by posing a systemic two-person psychology, with the session as a patient–analyst co-creation, a "complex of interacting transferences" imbued with "ambiguity and relativity of the interpersonal reality" (Gill, 1982). Today, on both sides of the Atlantic there is an increased recognition of Ferenczian intersubjective influences.

Submission to authority is an "escape from freedom", as Fromm was to say in 1941. Acclaiming his unique achievements, sympathetic commentators ultimately ascribe Ferenczi's liberation from adherence to Freud's theories (and especially that of genitality) to publication of *Thalassa* in 1924. However, this controversial book about the universal longing for prenatal existence, and sleep/coital return to the primal amniotic ocean was hailed by some of his contemporaries as evidence of mental instability. More recent critics claim it as a "poem" (Stanton, 1991, pp. 78–81), or conversely, as an extreme outburst of Haeckelian doctrine carried to "previously unimagined heights of folly" (Gould, 1977, p. 163). (This is Steven Jay Gould—who famously retorted to criticism of his own theory of sudden evolution as one defined by "jerks" by terming the opposition's view of slow change as "evolution by creeps".)

Conceived in the early years of his engagement with Freud, *Thalassa* remained dormant for almost ten years, until, as his 1923 introduction to the book proclaims, Ferenczi felt "emboldened by the acquisition of [this] insight" that "all physical and physiological phenomena require a *meta*-physical (i.e. psychological) explanation". Speculating on the ontogenetic recapitulation of phylogenetic development, slip-sliding symbolic linkages within the fertile womb of Ferenczi's imagination equate penis, child, and fish. The former, enveloped by a mucous membrane is threatened by castrative circumcision (as in his December 1912 dream of a cut off erect penis), but through potency regains entry to the womb in coitus, thus both undoing the expulsion of birth and replicating the aboriginal piscine mode (the fish as philogenetic aquatic ancestor of man). Furthermore, as the land-dwelling mammalian amnion shelters the foetus, the human female's twenty-eight-day cycle echoes the moon-drawn tide and her vaginal secretions retain their fishy odour, so the penis, as organ of copulation, retains the "memory" of the expulsion of the fish by the catastrophic drying up of the mother sea, repeated in the breaking of the waters in birth of a child. Commemorating this, the erect penis thus undoes the primal trauma of separation, reuniting sea, foetus, and fish, and, furthermore, in its tumescence, also recaptures the repose of the "era before life originated", "the deathlike repose of the inorganic world" (Ferenczi, 1924, p. 63).

To my mind, Hungarian title aside,[3] *Thalassa* smacks not of a cata-strophic break-down, or even break-through, but rather a brave *break-out*—a psychic "rebirth" after invigorating exploration of the life-giving maternal body by contrast to Freud's cautious circumnaviga-tion of the dangerous sepulchral maternal "casket" (the uncanny womb–tomb unconsciously identified with death, initially that of his own baby brother (Raphael-Leff, 1991)).

Perhaps recognising his courage, Freud had speedily "chosen" Sandor Ferenczi. In 1908, soon after their first meeting, he participated in the Viennese Society, was asked by Freud to give a paper at the first psychoanalytical congress in Salzburg, and invited to join Sigmund and his family on holiday in the German Bavarian Alps. Although local psychoanalytical groups were being formed in Zürich, Berlin, Munich, New York, and London, the Hungarian one was favoured.

Politically, Ferenczi was a democratic leader, serving both as President of the Hungarian Psychoanalytic Society until his death (with István Hollós as his deputy, and Sandor Radó as Secretary) and as President of the International Psycho-analytical Association—the IPA. Indeed, when, at the second conference in Nuremberg in 1910, Ferenczi proposed founding the IPA, he stressed (somewhat naïvely) his egalitarian ideal that

> [T]he psycho-analytically trained are surely the best adapted to found an association which would combine the greatest possible personal liberty with the advantage of family organization. It would be a family in which the father enjoyed no dogmatic authority . . . (Ferenczi, 1955[1911], p. 303)

and

> the older and younger children united in this association would ac-cept being told the truth to their face, however bitter and sobering it

might be, without childish sensitivity and vindictiveness. (Ferenczi, 1955[1911], p. 304)

(Today, the IPA numbers 12,000 members within seventy constituent organisations—see www.ipa.org.uk.)

Like the British Society's wide plurality of backgrounds, the Hungarian one aimed to be multi-disciplinary, as encouraged by Freud. However, this remained restricted, and, in 1927, when visiting New York, Ferenczi also lost a vigorous campaign for lay analysis with the American Psychoanalytic Association, a policy the APA finally did accept, but only in 1989.

Sandor was often regarded as an "impulsive sentimental . . . gypsy-music lover" (Thompson, 1988, p. 184). Numerous papers in this collection illuminate the unique contribution of his mother tongue and Hungarian culture to Ferenczi's psychoanalytic thinking. This included adherence to a vivacious lifestyle within a café-based network of artists and poets, musicians, and writers of fiction, plays, and short stories (a plurality that seems to echo the leftist intelligentsia of his parents' atmospheric bookshop).

But all across Europe these were heady days, with the fomentation of psychoanalytic explanatory models and ideas: proposing infantile sexuality, unmasking conscious supremacy, exposing discrepancies between overt puritanical morality and hidden or perverse behaviours, and exploring the intrapsychic conflicts of irrational desires, and so on. There were drawbacks, too, as the very few analysts analysed everyone with blithe disregard for familial relations, interconnections, and personal closeness. The risks of these brief treatments were residual transferential phenomena. Confidences crisscrossed boundaries, with little discretion about disguising patients. With scant consideration for professional decorum, analyses were conducted during evening walks in the Vienna Prater, continued during vacations in Bad Gastein or St Moritz, or even, in the case of Ferenczi and his superior officer, were literally conducted "on the trot", on horseback.

The fifth Psychoanalytic Congress (1918), held at the Academy of Sciences in Budapest, changed all that. Training analyses became a formal requirement (with Jones by Ferenczi being the first). Ferenczi was elected President of the IPA, replacing Abraham, and Freud earmarked Budapest as the future European epicentre of the psychoanalytic movement. It did flourish briefly as local psychoanalysts became involved in the newly formed Communist Party's plans for social reform, including a National Health Service. Shortly after his marriage in the spring of 1919, the Revolutionary Governing Council made Ferenczi the world's first Professor of Psychoanalysis, as part of training for doctors at Budapest Medical School. However, all that was reversed, as the Bolshevik revolution was rapidly followed by a right-wing dictatorship, and within two years the collapse of the Austro-Hungarian monarchy rendered Hungarian psychoanalysis subterranean, while institutional anti-Semitism flared up in the new authoritarian state. Expediently, the IPA Presidency was relinquished by Ferenczi to his ever-envious colleague and analysand, Ernest Jones.

A generous donation had been made by benefactor Antal von Tószeghi-Freund (aka Anton von Freund) to establish a low-fee psychoanalytic outpatient clinic in Budapest, to meet the post-war mass demand for psychotherapy foreseen by Freud. However, the donation was affected by the Hungarian economic instability, and the first *Poliklinik* was founded in Berlin in 1920, funded by Eitingon (alongside a training institute). Two years later, the Vienna free treatment *Ambulatorium* was opened with Hitschmann, and later Wilhelm Reich, as its Director. In 1924, Ferenczi declined Freud's invitation to move to Vienna to take over his Presidency of the Viennese Psychoanalytical Society and directorship of the Clinic. Due to a local government ban, it was 1931 before a similar polyclinic could be instituted in Budapest (which Ferenczi directed with Michael Balint as his deputy).

The 1920s saw the fermentation of a cultural revolution as psychologists, educators, social workers, the youth movement, and education departments of the Socialist parties began to soak up psychoanalytic ideas. Initially, the Vienna and Berlin clinics had included some provisions for non-physicians within their training programmes. However, possibly escalated by fears of Freud's impending death following the diagnosis of his cancer in 1923, psychoanalysis became appended to psychiatry. The Berlin Society now offered a complete teaching course to psychiatrists who agreed to first undergo a personal analysis (purged of didactic material) of at least six months' duration.

In July 1923, a celebratory edition of *Zeitschrift* was published to mark Ferenczi's fiftieth birthday. But xenophobia increased, partly due to Ferenczi's accusation of Berlin as "too theoretical", his revisions of psychoanalytic technique and the controversial unforeseen "dissident" publications by Rank and Ferenczi in 1924. Psychoanalytic orthodoxy solidified, and the selection process in Berlin came to encompass long trial periods, as training became more authoritarian.

At stake were disagreements around the primacy of Oedipal castration anxieties and intrapsychic conflicts, as opposed to the traumatogenic actuality of the early interactive environment. These differences led to divergent treatment techniques, with a split between advocates of interpretation leading to intellectual understanding and insight *vs.* a therapeutic "dialogue" with regression and emotional reliving at its core. The dispute was partly instigated by a new breed of patients. Those drawn to psychoanalytic treatment were no longer only neurotic hysterics, but more "basic fault" cases, abused, borderline, and traumatised people, hitherto neglected by psychoanalysis and necessitating modifications of classical approaches and an "elasticity of technique".

Gaining momentum, the theoretical divergence ripped across the closely interwoven psychoanalytic community. While continuing to pay lip service to Freud, increasingly Ferenczi's writings and work were seen to deviate markedly from the classical approach. During the last few years of his life, he became further alienated from critical colleagues. Given the charged atmosphere of secrecy, jealousy, envy, and rumour, details of the Freud–Ferenczi dispute at the web centre of this highly sensitive network were exaggerated as irreparable and catastrophic. None the less, their friendship survived, but culminated in pained dejection when, after discussion of previous drafts, Freud requested Ferenczi to abstain from delivering his paper "Confusion of tongues" at the 12th International Psychoanalytic Congress, and to replace it with another. Perceiving this as an attempt to suppress his views under the guise of concern for his reputation, outraged and hurt, Ferenczi proceeded to give his paper in Wiesbaden, to a hostile reception from many who saw it as discrediting psychoanalysis.

Already denounced for raising tension with his ascetic "active therapy", and then for relinquishing abstinence in his "rapport therapy", falsely accused of a "kissing technique", and also condemned for fostering dangerous intimacy and regression in analysis, "mutual analysis", self-disclosure, and calming "relaxation principles", Ferenczi now fell into total disfavour for reinstating the seduction theory, treating abuse allegations as real. He was further reviled for negating the idea of analyst as a blank screen, raising the spectre of "retraumatisation" of patients, and advocating acknowledgment of therapeutic errors.

Hurt to the core, despite his extraordinary personal capacity for lifelong growth and revision, Ferenczi's internal battle continued to rage, even in the very last note of his personal diary, written on 2 October 1932:

> Not yet being born is the danger . . . I had never really become 'grown up'. Scientific achievements, marriage, battles with formidable colleagues – all this was possible only under the protection of the idea that in all circumstances I can count on the father-surrogate . . . Is the only possibility for my continued existence the renunciation of the largest part of one's own self, in order to carry out the will of that higher power to the end (as though it were my own)? . . . Is the choice here one between dying and 'rearranging myself' . . . (Ferenczi, 1932, p. 212)

Ill with incurable pernicious anaemia but lucid (despite Jones' diagnosis of reactive psychosis), Ferenczi died on 22 May 1933, a few days before his sixtieth birthday. The man who had admitted "To be sure, I often make mistakes, but I am not rigid in my prejudices" (Falzeder & Brabant, 2000, p. 417) died in an atmosphere of utmost intolerance unseen since the Middle Ages, a fortnight after books written by Freud were publicly burned in Berlin as a "strong, great and symbolic deed", intended (in Goebbels' words) to end ". . . [T]he era of extreme Jewish intellectualism".

Today, there is a significant revival of interest in Ferenczi's work, which this volume addresses. Although countertransference, regression, dialogical unconscious influences, the metaphor of "maternal" therapeutic nurturing (and admission of mistakes) are now tacitly accepted by most psychoanalytically informed therapists, for many years following his death, Ferenczi's innovations went largely unrecognised or were ascribed to others. Among object relations, intersubjective, and relational theorists, Ferenczi is regarded as "the prescient innovator of all modern trends, champion of egalitarianism and mutuality, crusader for the recognition of child abuse and trauma" (Aron & Harris, 1993, p. 1).

Let us hail him as the emotionally attuned co-creator of psychoanalysis.

Notes

1. Jones, Rank, Sachs, Abraham, and, later, Eitingon.
2. Pen-name of Hugo Veigelsberg.
3. The exact Hungarian title is *Katasztrófák a nemi működés fejlődésében*: that is, "Catastrophes in the development of sexual function".

References

Aron, L. & Harris, A. (1993). Sándor Ferenczi. Discovery and rediscovery. In: L. Aron & A. Harris (Eds.), *The Legacy of Sándor Ferenczi* (pp. 1–36). Hillsdale, NJ: Analytic Press.

Ashbery, J. (1979). *Late Echo*. London: Penguin Books.

Balbernie, R. (2001). Circuits and circumstances: the neurobiological consequences of early relationship experiences and how they shape later behaviour. *Journal of Child Psychotherapy*, *27*: 237–255.

Balint, M. (1933). Sándor Ferenczi, Obituary. *International Journal of Psychoanalysis*, *30*: 215–219.

Beebe, B., & Lachman, F. (2002). *Infant Research and Adult Treatment: Co-constructing Interactions*. London: Analytic Press.

Bucci, W. (2002). The referential process, consciousness, and the sense of self. *Psychoanalytic Inquiry*, *22*: 766–793.

Falzeder, E. (Ed.) (2002). *The Complete Correspondence of Sigmund Freud and Karl Abraham 1907–1925* (pp. 162–163). London: Karnac, 2002.

Falzeder, E., & Brabant E. (Eds.) (1996). *The Correspondence of Sigmund Freud and Sándor Ferenczi Volume 2, 1914–1919*. Cambridge, MA: Harvard University Press.

Falzeder, E., & Brabant, E. (Eds.) (2000). *The Correspondence of Sigmund Freud and Sándor Ferenczi Volume 3, 1920–1933*. Cambridge, MA: Harvard University Press.

Ferenczi, S. (1911). On the organisation of the psycho-analytic movement. In: M. Balint (Ed.), E. Mosbacher & others (Trans.), *Final Contributions to the Problems and Methods of Psycho-Analysis* (pp. 299–315). London: Hogarth Press, 1955 [reprinted, London: Karnac, 1994].

Ferenczi, S. (1924). *Thalassa: A Theory of Genitality*. London: Karnac, 1984.

Ferenczi, S. (1926). Preface. In: J. Rickman (Ed.), J. I. Suttie & others (Trans.), *Further Contributions to the Theory and Technique of Psycho-Analysis* (pp. 7–9). London: Hogarth Press, 1926 [reprinted, London: Hogarth Press, 1955 & London: Karnac, 1994].

Ferenczi, S. (1932). *The Clinical Diary of Sándor Ferenczi*, J. Dupont (Ed.), M. Balint & N. Z. Jackson (Trans.). Cambridge, MA: Harvard University Press, 1988.

Ferenczi, S. (1933). Confusion of tongues between adults and the child. In: *Final Contributions to the Problems and Methods of Psycho-Analysis* (pp. 156–167). London: Hogarth Press, 1955 [reprinted, London: Karnac, 1994].

Ferenczi, S. (1955). *Final Contributions to the Problems and Methods of Psycho-Analysis*, M. Balint (Ed.), E. Mosbacher & others (Trans.). London: Hogarth Press, 1955 [reprinted, London: Karnac, 1994].

Fortune, C. (Ed.) (2002). *The Sándor Ferenczi–Georg Groddeck Correspondence, 1921–1933*. London: Open Gate Press.

Fromm, E. (1941). *Escape From Freedom*. New York: Rinehart.

Gerhardt, S. (2004). *Why Love Matters: How Affection Shapes a Baby's Brain*. London: Psychology Press.

Gill, M. M. (1982). *Analysis of Transference*. New York: International Universities Press.

Gould, S. J. (1977). *Ontogeny and Phylogeny*. Cambridge, MA: Harvard University Press.

Heimann, P. (1950). On counter-transference. *International Journal of Psychoanalysis*, 31: 81–84.

Raphael-Leff, J. (1986). Facilitators and Regulators: conscious and unconscious processes in pregnancy and early motherhood. *British Journal of Medical Psychology*, 59: 43–55.

Raphael-Leff, J. (1991). *Psychological Processes of Childbearing*. Colchester: CPS Psychoanalytical Publications Series.

Raphael-Leff, J. (2012). The intersubjective matrix: influences on the Independents' growth from "object-relations" to "subject-relations". In: P. Williams, J. Keene, & S. Dermen (Eds.), *Independent Analysis Today* (pp. 87–162). London: Karnac.

Schore, A. N. (2001). The effects of early relational trauma on right-brain development, affect regulation, and infant mental health. *Infant Mental Health Journal*, 22: 201–269.

Stanton, M. (1991). *Sándor Ferenczi: Reconsidering Active Intervention*. Northvale, NJ: Jason Aronson.

Thompson, C. M. (1988). Sándor Ferenczi, 1873–1933. *Contemporary Psychoanalysis*, 24: 182–195.

PART I
MELANIE KLEIN AND SANDOR FERENCZI

From patient to founder of a psychoanalytic school: Ferenczi's influence on the works of Melanie Klein

Gábor Flaskay

Nobody within the psychoanalytic community doubts that Melanie Klein was one of the most influential contributors to our discipline after the first great generation of psychoanalysts. Her findings on the early mental development of the child and the derived theoretical conclusions have had a great impact on general psychoanalytical theories and practice.

Life and work of Melanie Klein (1882–1960)

Melanie Klein was born in Vienna in 1882. She married in 1903 and moved to Rózsahegy (Rosenberg, Ruzomberok), a small town in the region of the Austro-Hungarian monarchy with a Hungarian, Slovak, German, and Jewish population. She became acquainted with the languages spoken there. She had an unhappy marriage, with significant periods of separation, and she divorced in 1922.

Klein moved to Budapest in 1910 and enjoyed the intellectual vitality of the "big town". Sandor Ferenczi saw her for the first time in 1912, in order to treat her depression. Her sporadic visits to Ferenczi's office were changed to a formal psychoanalytic treatment

A glamorous young Melanie Klein.

in 1914; soon after that, Ferenczi was called up to serve in the army, stationed 120 km away from Budapest. He visited Budapest occasionally and continued sporadic analysis with his analysands (including Géza Róheim and Klein). Ferenczi was transferred back to Budapest in 1916.

Melanie Klein encountered Freud's work in Budapest, and she attended the meetings of the Hungarian Psychoanalytical Society from 1914 onwards. The meetings were a kind of social encounter, in which members of the Society were accompanied by their family members and those who were interested in this new approach. Klein remained in analysis with Ferenczi until 1919. In that year, she became a member of the Hungarian Psychoanalytical Society after presenting her paper, "The development of a child", to the membership of the Society.

Ferenczi suggested to Klein that she closely observe children as a means of approaching her own problems. Later, he proposed that she treat children using psychoanalysis.

At the Hague Congress in 1920, Ferenczi introduced Klein to Abraham. In 1921, Klein moved to Berlin, where she became a well-known child analyst some years later. She was in contact with Ferenczi through letters. Her creativity and originality soon appeared. In 1924, Klein started analysis with Abraham: it lasted for about eight months, until Abraham's early death.

Ernest Jones invited Klein to move to London. He wanted to strengthen the British Society with her presence and, secondarily, he wanted to have an appropriate analyst for his children. Klein arrived in London in 1927. By that time her technique of child analysis was fully worked out and her original contribution was in progress. This resulted in her book, *The Psychoanalysis of Children*, published in 1932, a work which Edward Glover considered a milestone in the development of psychoanalysis.

She followed the tradition of the Hungarian School of Psychoanalysis (Ferenczi, Balint) when she emphasised the significance of the object in the psychological development of the child. She was among the founders of the British object relations theory. She presumed that the early external object relations became internal within the realm of unconscious phantasy and would be components of the personality, determining the later social and transferential relations. She described the process of "psychological metabolism" through introjection and projection.

The paranoid–schizoid and depressive positions are lucid constellations of drives, objects, and defences widely used in psychoanalytic understanding nowadays. The description of defences characteristic of these positions opened new ways of understanding certain psychopathologies. Her discoveries of the influence of early strivings and anxieties on the development of the Oedipus complex are also fundamental.

Klein's work resulted in a basic development of psychoanalytic technique, in which more emphasis was put on work with transference and pregenital processes. What is absolutely certain is that psychoanalysis today would not be the same without the contributions made by Melanie Klein.

Melanie Klein's work relies on the findings of three outstanding masters—Freud, Ferenczi, and Abraham—and on the personal impact of the latter two.

Freud

The importance of Freud is obvious. He invented the whole method and described its metapsychology; he laid down the theoretical foundations of the science and art of psychoanalysis. He constantly reviewed his new approach and updated it in the light of new find-ings, thus establishing the practice of psychoanalysis. Freud was a real scientist in the sense that he was driven by the motivation of scientific cognition throughout his work. He was interested in the fate of the instincts in the lives of human beings; how—through what processes and intermediate states—do compromises evolve between satisfaction of the instincts and forces prohibiting such satisfactions? As Haynal, quoting what Freud had told Klein, wrote, "I am interested only in unconscious" (Haynal, 1989, p. 3). When Klein drew attention to the observation that the functioning of instincts is manifested in their rela-tionship to psychological objects, and that it makes no sense to talk about instincts without those objects, it meant a conceptual change in the field of psychoanalysis. In her own words,

> The analysis of very young children has taught me that there is no instinctual urge, no anxiety situation, no mental process which does not involve objects, external or internal: in other words, object-rela-tions are the centre of emotional life. Furthermore, love and hatred, phantasies, anxieties and defences are also operative from the begin-ning of life. (Klein, 1952, p. 53)

Abraham

Karl Abraham was a great contributor to the formation of Melanie Klein's concept of object-relations, calling attention to the significance of the pregenital period, and the part-objects within it, which have a great role in the process of personality development. By establishing the object-relations theory, Klein essentially questioned one of the basic principles of Freud: the principle of primary narcissism. It is important to stress this difference because this is the basic character-istic of the so-called Budapest School of Psychoanalysis, or Hungarian School of Psychoanalysis. The students of Ferenczi—Michael Balint, Alice Balint, Imre Hermann and, in this respect, Melanie Klein as well—agreed pretty much that the newborn is not only a physiologi-cal being in the beginning, but an active object-seeking person who turns to the primary object or part-objects (Klein) with affects.

It was a great help for Klein to have discovered relatively early the psychoanalytic play technique. The play technique not only revolutionised the practice of child analysis, but also widened greatly the spectrum in which we can recognise and treat transference, through the description of the two positions and of the early emotions and defence mechanisms functioning within those positions. In this way, the method of psychoanalysis could be extended to cases of severely regressed patients, who were considered untreatable by Freud's method of psychoanalysis. It turned out that such patients were also able to produce transference, with the difference that their transference was of pregenital nature, and, thus, in its appearance basically different from the Oedipal type of transference. Klein's object-relations theory—with active internalised objects within unconscious phantasies and the early anxieties that influence the development of the Oedipal situation—provides indispensable elements of psychoanalytic knowledge today (Flaskay, 1983).

Melanie Klein in Budapest

Until psychoanalysis appeared in Melanie Klein's life and enabled her to take a new direction, many things had happened to her. Her adulthood started early, at the age of seventeen, with a long process of engagement, followed by an unhappy marriage. Her first child was soon born. Her early engagement and marriage prevented her from finishing her academic education. Signs of her depression appeared soon after her marriage. Her mother often spoke about Melanie's "unfortunate nerves". In a letter of 25 April 1906, she wrote to her daughter, "It is your fate or, unfortunately, your disposition that there is always something that tortures you" (Grosskurth, 1987). During one of her travels to be cured in Abbazia (now Opatia) on the Adriatic coast, she met Klára Vágó, a distant relative of her husband. Klára Vágó was an intelligent, educated, and independent woman; she was also a divorced woman, a rarity at that time. A strong friendship developed between them, and she became a kind of "mother-substitute" for Melanie.

Melanie Klein's first visit to Budapest occurred after an invitation from Klára Vágó offering her the possibility of taking a rest there. Thus, when Melanie Klein actually moved to Budapest in 1910 with her family, she did not encounter an altogether unfamiliar place. She had acquaintances there and she knew the city as well. Budapest was experiencing the most favourable period of its history in 1910: many would call this period the "Golden Age". The Austro-Hungarian Compromise (*Ausgleich*) of 1867 had brought peace and political stability to the country. It was followed by unprecedented economic development and boom, which assured the economic basis for the 1896 celebration of the first millennium of the Hungarian Kingdom and state. Impressive public buildings were erected and grand bridges, railway stations, and Continental Europe's first underground train system were built. All these were accompanied by a thrilling atmosphere of a vivid scientific and cultural life. Literary salons were common and high-quality journals appeared regularly. It was not by chance that Budapest, a cultural capital of Europe in those days, was one of the first among the European cities to accept and host psychoanalysis, the new doctrine and paradigm.

Medical journals and publications collected and published the writings of Freud, Ferenczi, and other psychoanalysts. It is well documented in literary works, fiction, essays, and memoirs that psychoanalysis was at the core of debates and discussions among intellectuals, and that it attracted interest and enjoyed popularity as a topic of discussion in cafés and salons. In May 1913, Ferenczi founded the Hungarian Psychoanalytical Association with five members.

When Melanie Klein arrived in Budapest she was in a difficult and desperate life situation. It had ultimately become clear to her that her marriage with Arthur Klein did not work. Moving in with her mother brought to the surface the ambivalence in their relationship, which had existed from the very beginning. According to her biographer, Grosskurth (1987), ". . . Melanie's feelings of hostility towards Arthur are indisputable, and seem to be fused with unconscious hatred towards her mother" (p. 69). She lost her mother in 1914. After several attempts at separation, she divorced her husband ten years later.

Melanie Klein learnt Hungarian in Rózsahegy (today's Slovakia)— where she had lived before—and Budapest, and regularly attended the meetings of the Hungarian Psychoanalytical Association from 1914 onward. Those meetings had a fairly relaxed atmosphere; family members, friends, and acquaintances were also allowed to be present. Allegedly, Melitta (later Melitta Schmideberg), the daughter of Melanie Klein, also attended these meetings in 1919, at the age of fifteen (Harmat, 1994).

Klein's analysis with Ferenczi

Available pieces of information concerning when and under what circumstances Melanie Klein met Ferenczi and was introduced to psychoanalysis are ambiguous. It is certain, however, that such an encounter must have taken place during her stay in Budapest. In her autobiography, she mentions that in 1914 she came across and read *Über den Traum*, by Freud. She indicates that this text inspired her to start an analysis with Ferenczi, "the most outstanding Hungarian analyst". Other biographers of Klein suggest that she had begun to see Ferenczi, "the best nerve specialist", regularly, as early as 1912 (Grosskurth, 1987; Dupont, quoted in Harmat, 1994). Harmat, on the other hand, specifies the year 1916 as the beginning of Klein's analysis (1994, p. 336).

Psychoanalysis meant something different to Ferenczi than it meant to Freud. (It is reported that Freud once told Melanie Klein, "I am interested only in the unconscious".) Ferenczi conceived of psychoanalysis as a tool with which one could help other suffering people. He himself wrote,

> I have had a kind of fanatical belief in the efficacy of depth-psychology, and this has led me to attribute occasional failures not so much to the patient's 'incurability' as to our own lack of skill. . . . It is thus only with the utmost reluctance that I ever bring myself to give up even the most obstinate cases, with which I go on for very many years. I have refused to accept such verdicts as that a patient's resistance was unconquerable, or that his narcissism prevented our penetrating any further or the sheer fatalistic acquiescence in the so-called 'drying up' of a case. (Ferenczi, 1931, p. 128)

It did happen that his great benevolent endeavour to help someone took Ferenczi off course and led him astray; however, once he had recognised his mistake, he was never reluctant to change. This is well illustrated by his experiences with mutual analysis.

It is the generally shared view of Melanie Klein's analysis with Ferenczi that there was something wrong with it: it did not proceed as an analysis ought to proceed. According to her biographers, the major problem of Melanie Klein's analysis was that Ferenczi ignored the negative transference; he failed to analyse it, idealised his patient, and performed an incomplete job. Melanie Klein herself, however, says something else in this connection: her formulation is much more refined, "Technique at this time was extremely different from what it is at present and the analysis of negative transference did not enter" (Grosskurth, 1987). It seems very much to be the case that many people make Ferenczi accountable for not having used some method (transference) that was not part of the everyday practice of psycho-analytic treatment of his day, though it had been discussed in some writings. As a matter of fact, Ferenczi had actually made much greater progress in the understanding and treatment of transference than most of his contemporaries.

There are different answers to the question of what the reasons could have been for criticism and why ignorance persisted for so long in Ferenczi's judgement, which are dealt with in more detail in other chapters of the present volume. Here is a brief list of some of them: Ferenczi's negative transference with Freud, which came out in their disputes as well; Ferenczi's rational criticism toward some views and the therapeutic attitude of Freud, to which Freud often reacted sensi-tively and sometimes even rejectively; the traumatisation of the psychoanalytic community because of the conflict between Freud and Ferenczi (Balint, cited in Haynal, 1989), the result of which was that the followers identified with Freud, dissociating themselves from the "dissident" Ferenczi out of fear that dissidents could jeopardise the unity and stability of the group (Melanie Klein was later also consid-ered a "dissident"); the jealousy and rivalry of Jones toward Ferenczi, in which many took sides with Jones; Ferenczi's active technique and his concept of mutual analysis, which indeed surpasses the frame-work of psychoanalysis in several respects; and, as a last remark, the accent or weight attributed to Sandor Ferenczi in writings dealing with the background of, and precursors to, the work of Melanie Klein.

I want to focus on the influences Ferenczi might have exerted on the development of Klein's views and findings. Some of the authors analysing the work of Klein underestimated Ferenczi, as was the general tendency of the day. These authors tended to devalue the importance of Ferenczi in Melanie Klein's professional development, in highly refined but consistent ways. This might be related to some of the conditions referred to above; however, it is most probably a consequence of the Ferenczi imago emanating from, and transmitted by, Jones. (As we know, Jones consistently stood beside Klein in great storms and supported her against Freud.) It is very difficult to judge what role Melanie Klein's loyalty to Jones might have played in the way she herself remembers Ferenczi.

Taking into consideration the above mentioned observations and not denying certain specificities of Ferenczi's character that might have influenced the relationship between himself and Melanie Klein, it is also worth mentioning a number of objective facts, which might have influenced the process of Klein's analysis with Ferenczi and her feelings during and after the analysis. In 1914, when her analysis began (according to most of her biographers), the First World War broke out and Ferenczi was drafted. As mentioned before, he was assigned to medical service 120 kilometres from Budapest. According to records, he visited Budapest often and saw his patients. However, this situation, which lasted for two years, must have caused quite a lot of frustration to his patients.

Melanie Klein's analysis with Ferenczi ended in 1919 under circumstances as difficult as when it began. The end of the First World War and the fall of the Austro-Hungarian Monarchy was followed by tremendous social tension in Hungary. Budapest witnessed a Bolshevik revolution and take-over in the same year, which soon spread all over the country. Its consequence was a merciless Bolshevik terror. In order to assure security for her children and herself, Melanie Klein fled to their former home, Rózsahegy (today's Ruzomberok in Slovakia), where her husband's parents lived. (At that time Rózsahegy already belonged to Czechoslovakia.) The Bolshevik terror did not last long after the move, but was immediately followed by the White Terror, with its retaliations. A few years later, the continuation of her analysis took place in Berlin with Karl Abraham; but was discontinued under tragic circumstances—the sudden death of Abraham. It is not impossible that this tragic event also affected, retrospectively, Melanie Klein's feelings toward Ferenczi.

Ferenczi's influence

In 1919, Melanie Klein left Budapest and Ferenczi, and after a short detour, ended up in Berlin. She had left behind the rather difficult first part of her life and, identifying with her new calling, began a new life. She felt she was doing the right thing, for which she soon received recognition. From the record of her life, it can be seen that the major part of her depression had been left behind in Budapest with Ferenczi. After Budapest, there are no traces in her biographical writings that she would have needed a rest of several months as in the past, which, in the fashion of the times, would have been the treatment offered, for her mood disturbances. In 1924, she entered Abraham's consulting room as a known child analyst, and as a colleague who wanted to learn from an outstanding expert.

Whatever her analysis with Ferenczi might have been like in Budapest, there is good reason to believe and assume that Melanie Klein had "found herself" in Budapest, with the help of Ferenczi; after that, her life took a radical turn. She entered a therapeutic profession, which she had longed for ever since she was a child, even though it had taken a detour to get there. By practising this profession, she could satisfy her intellectual thirst and get an insight into the deeper strata of human motivations. With the fulfillment of her professional career, she greatly contributed to the development of the theory and practice of psychoanalysis.

Nobody denies that Ferenczi was the one who encouraged Melanie Klein to start her analytical work with children. He was Klein's first informal supervisor. Their correspondence witnesses that Ferenczi advised her what literature to read and later introduced her into the international analytical community. In the beginning, Melanie Klein did indeed need the support of Ferenczi. At the Hague Congress in 1920, the only child analyst of that time, Hermine von Hug-Hellmuth, was not even willing to talk to Klein, her new rival. And soon another rival appeared: Anna Freud. The first significant creative contribution of Melanie Klein was the development of the analytic play technique. Ferenczi was enthusiastic about it and acknowledged its importance in several of his writings. Later, in his work "Child-analysis in the analysis of adults" (Ferenczi, 1931), in which explicit reference was made to Klein, the impact of the child analytic method can be recognised.

Ferenczi's main aim in his paper is to diminish the widely believed difference between child analysis and that of the adult. He states that in order to entirely explore a case, the early childhood traumas have to appear in the analytic situation. (This is also one of the fundamental principles of Klein.) However, those traumas are often revealed via non-verbal means, through a certain child-like behaviour in the analytic situation. Thus, as Ferenczi puts it, his analyses often turned into a kind of child's play. In other words, infantile acting-out appeared in his analyses; Ferenczi allowed this to evolve like the various games in child analysis and then tried to process the events with the method of Klein's play technique. This technique is well reflected in Ferenczi's own words:

> Not infrequently patients, often in the middle of their free association, produce little stories which they have made up, or even poems and rhymes, and sometimes they ask for a pencil so as to make us a present of a drawing, generally of a very naive sort. Naturally I let them indulge in this and make the little gifts a starting-point for further phantasy-formations which I afterwards analyse. Does not this by itself sound as if it came from the analysis of children? (Ferenczi, 1931, p. 133)

Regression was thought of by both Ferenczi and Klein as the necessary constituent of the analytical process. Here, however, comes the important difference between the view held by Ferenczi and that of Klein: the way each of them treated the regressive situation and the regressive transference. Among Ferenczi's tools there was a place for tactful, calming words and, beyond these, a friendly touch of the shoulder. Klein kept the original Freudian attitude, which aimed at rigorously maintaining the psychoanalytic setting so as to keep the transference as pure and uncontaminated as possible. This attitude is based on a belief that the transference situation is active from the very beginning of the analysis, and the interpretation is the most important therapeutic element; the interpretation is of anxiety and defence together, rather than either on its own. Today, when we know a lot more about transference and countertransference, I believe there are only a few analysts who would follow Ferenczi's original method for patients with severe regression. It becomes more and more clear, however, that the analyst's activity and striving in the cases of such patients yield much better chances for successful analysis than passive waiting. However, some of us would dispute Kernberg's view about stalemates with patients with severe personality disorders, that ". . . it is better for the therapist to risk becoming a 'bull in a china shop' than to remain paralysed, lulled into passive collusion with the patient's destruction of time" (Kernberg, 1984, p. 245). All of us have experienced that sometimes non-interpretative elements can help analysis out of stalemates.

In Melanie Klein's conception, transference receives a much greater role than it had earlier. Klein (1952) introduced the concept of total transference: in the analytic situation, it is not simply certain desires, anxieties, and emotions that are projected on to the analyst, but total situations from the past are transferred into the analytic situation, together with emotions, their defence mechanisms, and early object relationships. Klein's followers have kept this concept and complemented it with a greater emphasis on countertransference, aiming at holistic or integrative interpretations.

Transference also played a great role in the work of Ferenczi. Ferenczi first met Freud in 1908, and essentially this is when he began to be involved in psychoanalysis. A year later, he had already made one of his important discoveries in the context of transference: he described the phenomenon of introjection, in which the ego widens its interests toward parts of the external world—that is, the ego incorporates elements of the external world into itself. He describes "psychological metabolism", the dynamic relation of introjection and projection, which later on will become an important part of Klein's metapsychology when she defines the basis of personality in terms of the system of internal objects within unconscious phantasies. In this work of 1909, Ferenczi defines the most important effect factor in psychoanalytical therapy (which Freud and others make more precise): the neurotic patient, no matter how he is treated, reaches his therapy through transference. "The origins of transference" are, according to Ferenczi, the first "object love" and the first "object hate" (Ferenczi, 1909, in 1952, p. 49). Haynal writes that Ferenczi greatly expanded the concept of transference. He cites Ferenczi: "I regard every dream, every gesture, every parapraxis, every aggravation or improvement in the condition of a patient above all an expression of transference and resistance" (Ferenczi, 1926, p. 225, cited in Haynal, 1989, p. 16). I think that this kind of treatment of transference is a good basis for the development of the holistic transference approach.

In Melanie Klein's model of personality development and in her theory on psychopathology formation, splitting plays an important role. The first description of splitting originated with Freud. He observed splitting, in cases of fetishism and psychosis, as a disturbance in relation to reality. The ego splits itself so that there is one part, the normal ego, which takes account of reality, and another that, under the influence of the instincts, detaches itself from reality (Freud, 1927e).

Coincidentally, Freud and Ferenczi observed the phenomenon of splitting at roughly the same time. Ferenczi's contribution to splitting is also important. He first mentions it in 1927, as a developmental deficiency in which the different parts of the personality, especially the aspects of the superego, have failed to fuse, resulting in uncertainty and inconsistent behaviour (Ferenczi, 1955, p. 78). (Later he mentions splitting in the elaboration of trauma, in which this phenomenon is indicated basically as a defence mechanism to protect the personality from the total burden of the trauma.) In his 1931 formulation, Ferenczi's notion of splitting is very close to the way in which Melanie Klein treats the phenomenon of splitting in her theory of object-relations. Ferenczi wrote,

> If in the analytic situation the patient feels hurt, disappointed, or left in the lurch, he sometimes begins to play by himself like a lonely child. One definitely gets the impression that to be left deserted results in a split of personality. Part of the person adopts the role of father or mother in relation to the rest, thereby undoing, as it were, the fact of being left deserted. (Ferenczi, 1931, p. 135)

Ferenczi, however, does not stop there. With the phenomenon of splitting as his basis, he arrives at the initial definition of idealisation, which gained great importance in Klein's object-relations theory as a defence mechanism. Concerning the traumatised child, he writes,

> If the child had not been loved before or had even been tortured, then he splits a part from himself which is helpful and loving, which takes pity on the ill-treated remains of his personality as a mother takes care of and takes the responsibility of her child, doing all this with the greatest of wisdom, and overwhelming sense and intelligence. This phenomenon is intelligence and goodness itself, we could say it is a patron-saint. (Ferenczi, 1933, p. 451)

I would like to mention one more important aspect of Ferenczi's discoveries, which was further pursued by Melanie Klein and constitutes a substantial part of her conceptual system. This is the elaboration of trauma and the creative behaviour connected to it. Briefly, Ferenczi believes that a consequence of trauma is that the strong shock results in a split of the personality; one part of the personality suffers the traumatic experience while the other takes on the role of an observer. The traumatised part goes into a state of psychological death through the process of "primary repression", thus protecting its entire self from the effect of trauma. The patient can be cured if the analysis reaches to this deep, dead part and revives it by analysing it during the re-living of the trauma in the analytic situation. (Ferenczi, 1934) According to Ferenczi, this work initiates valuable creative behaviour in many individuals.

Melanie Klein arrives at a similar conclusion when she analyses the process taking place in the realm of unconscious phantasies in the depressive position. The "destructive" elements of personality—part of which are inborn and part of which are strengthened through frustration—destroy the personality's inner good objects, the positive nucleus, leaving behind emotions of hopelessness and depression. Analysis helps to revive the destroyed inner good objects, giving way to reparative tendencies and, thus, establishing a favourable situation for creative behaviour (Flaskay, 1992).

References

Ferenczi, S. (1909). Introjection and transference. In: *First Contribution to Psycho-Analysis by Sándor Ferenczi* (pp. 35–93). London: Hogarth Press, 1952 [reprinted, London: Karnac, 1994].

Ferenczi, S. (1926). Contra-indications to the 'active' psycho-analytical technique. In: *Further Contributions to the Theory and Technique of Psycho-Analysis* (pp. 217–230), J. Rickman (Ed.), J. I. Suttie & others (Trans.). London: Hogarth Press, 1926 [reprinted, London: Hogarth Press, 1955; London: Karnac, 1994].

Ferenczi, S. (1927). The problem of termination of the analysis. In: *Final Contributions to the Problems and Methods of Psycho-Analysis* (pp. 77–86), M. Balint (Ed.), E. Mosbacher & others (Trans.). London: Hogarth Press, 1955 [reprinted, London: Karnac, 1994.

Ferenczi, S. (1931). Child-analysis in the analysis of adults. In: *Final Contributions to the Problems and Methods of Psycho-Analysis* (pp. 126–142), M. Balint (Ed.), E. Mosbacher & others (Trans.). London: Hogarth Press, 1955 [reprinted, London: Karnac, 1994].

Ferenczi, S. (1933). Confusion of tongues between adults and the child. In: *Final Contributions to the Problems and Methods of Psycho-Analysis* (pp. 156–167), M. Balint (Ed.), E. Mosbacher & others (Trans.). London: Hogarth Press, 1955 [reprinted, London: Karnac, 1994].

Ferenczi, S. (1934). Trauma a pszichoanalízisben (Trauma in psycho-analysis) in *Lelki problémák a pszichoanalízis tükrében. Válogatás Ferenczi Sándor tanulmányaiból* (pp. 139–452). Budapest: Magvető Kiadó, 1982.

Ferenczi, S. (1955). *Final Contributions to the Problems and Methods of Psycho-Analysis*, M. Balint (Ed.), E. Mosbacher & others (Trans.). London: Hogarth Press, 1955 [reprinted, London: Karnac, 1994].

Flaskay, G. (1983). Melanie Klein elméleti és technikai újításai az anali-tikus pszichoterápiában. *Magyar Pszichológiai Szemle* (Melanie Klein's theoretical and technical innovations in analytical psychotherapy. *Review of Hungarian Psychology*), 40(2): 119–133.

Flaskay, G. (1992). A depresszió tárgykapcsolati megközelítése. In: *Klinikai pszichológiai szöveggy_jtemény* (An object-relational approach of de-pression. In: Collected Papers in Clinical Psychology) (pp. 168–175). Budapest:Tankönyvkiadó.

Freud, S. (1927e). Fetishism. *S.E., 21*: 147–157. London: Hogarth.

Grosskurth, P. (1987). *Melanie Klein, Her World and Her Work*. Cambridge, MA: Harvard University Press.

Harmat, P. (1994). *Freud, Ferenczi és a magyarországi pszichoanalízis* (Freud, Ferenczi and Psychoanalysis in Hungary). Budapest: Bethlen Gábor.

Haynal, A. (1989). *Controversies in Psychoanalytic Method*, E. Holder (Trans.). New York: New York University Press.

Kernberg, O. (1984). *Severe Personality Disorders*. New Haven, CT: Yale University Press.

Klein, M. (1952). The origins of transference. In: *Envy And Gratitude And Other Works, 1946–1963. The Writings of Melanie Klein, Vol. 3* (pp. 48–56). London: Hogarth Press, 1975.

CHAPTER TWO

The "here-and-now" in Ferenczi's thinking and its influence on Melanie Klein

Meira Likierman

T he influence of Ferenczi upon Melanie Klein was obviously complex, and is best understood in the context of their analytic and mentoring relationship. In this respect, it involved far more than Klein's acquisition of a handful of concepts. Ferenczi did indeed pass on to Klein both concepts and themes, which she then went on to develop.

However, I would like to look at Ferenczi's influence more broadly, and think of it as arising from a multi-layered contact between them. Both personal and analytic aspects of Ferenczi influenced Klein—his cherished beliefs, his unique personal idiom, and his overall vision of mental life. I am assuming that these more personal elements were absorbed by Klein in unconscious, and not only in conscious, ways. Elements of Ferenczi's thinking are, thus, apparent, not just at the beginning of Klein's career, when she was still in contact with him, but are also reflected throughout her complete life's work, well after their contact ceased (Likierman, 2001).

I can select only a few examples, but one example that comes to mind, which I have already explored more extensively, was the impact on Klein's overall theory of Ferenczi's paper "Stages in the development of the sense of reality" (1913). The thesis of this paper presents psychic development as hinging on the move from omnipotence to reality—originally a Freudian idea. But Ferenczi elaborated its implications for child development and showed it to be a process that is protracted over the entire period of early childhood, with several stages. Thus, he emphasised the difficulty, for each individual, of abandoning a sheltered omnipotent position and choosing to live with a sense of reality. Ferenczi's careful phrasing indicates that the individual never acquires a full knowledge of reality, only a "sense" of it.

In this Ferenczi-inspired form, the essence of the idea passed on to Klein survived through the many permutations of her evolving theory, and is taken for granted in her most complex papers. For example, her idea of the epistemophilic instinct, a kind of instinct for knowledge, accounted for a force that draws the developing child away from omnipotent phantasy towards a reality-seeking existence. As with Ferenczi, this reality is not a simple undistorted external reality. It also has a twofold expression: worldly events acquire significance by virtue of being vested with subjective phantasy, but there is an internal reality that can be sensed, and that is sought during development. In optimal conditions, the developing individual learns to discover and accept the reality of his own human nature, and live thereafter with a sense of it. Today, we would think in terms of fluctuations in a person's choice to sense more of internal reality, or to retreat from what is sensed. I believe that without this idea it is not possible to appreciate fully Klein's major papers on the paranoid–schizoid and depressive positions, which contain her vision of development.

We see several aspects of Ferenczi's influence in Klein's first psychoanalytic project in more direct ways. This project was the analytic education, and later the analysis, of her son Eric when he was four and a half. Unlike Freud's case of Little Hans, Klein was not setting out to treat a child who had succumbed to a nervous condition, but to prevent the child's future pathology, which would develop if certain current aspects of his behaviour were not addressed in good time. Eric, described by her as "healthy and alert" was academically slow, and seemed to have obstacles that prevented the development of a healthy enquiring attitude, exactly the curiosity and love of knowledge that Klein prized so much. She worried that, without treatment, he would suffer what she called an "intellectual injury" (Klein, 1921, in 1975, p. 19). In the seminal writing where Klein described her work with her son, it is possible to see Ferenczi's far-reaching influence over a whole range of ideas.

The paper uses assumptions from "Stages in the development of the sense of reality" in following Eric's struggle between his omnipotent urges and his need to adapt to the world. But this Ferenczi-inspired psychoanalytic understanding of the child represents only one dimension of Klein's paper. In its other dimension, the paper turns from the consulting room outward to the world and becomes a manifesto for a new kind of child rearing. Klein boldly advocates a new openness with children that could revolutionise family life: "Honesty towards children, frank answering of their questions, and the inner freedom which this brings about, influence mental development profoundly and beneficially" (Klein, 1921, in 1975, p. 19).

In this thinking, sexuality would become free from what Klein described as "dense veils of secrecy". The natural "wishes, thoughts and feelings" of the child do not become a "burden of false shame and nervous suffering". Klein's paper shows that the repressive tool which adults use against children is religion, and she struggles throughout her analysis of Eric to wean him off religious beliefs and turn his mind to rationality and reality. The entire thrust of Klein's first project reflects Ferenczi's views on the education and rearing of children. He believed that the conventional education of his day could be harmful, especially if it proceeded through "the repression of emotions and ideas" (Ferenczi, 1908, cited in Petot, 1990, p. 21), or worse, through the "the negation of emotions and ideas" (p. 21). He suggested that "moralizing education based on repression calls forth a modicum of neurosis even in the healthy" (p. 22).

In Ferenczi's view, the main instrument for a tyrannical intellectual suppression of children used by adults was religion. Ferenczi's thinking was in keeping with other progressive currents in European intellectual life, but he was no doubt attacking the educational system of his day in Budapest and parts of eastern and central Europe, where religion and superstition still held sway. He cited for comparison countries such as France, which had removed the catechism from the school curriculum, and instead introduced the child to a civic value system via "an elementary book which gives the child his first instruction in his position as citizen" (Ferenczi, 1908, cited in Petot, 1990, p. 22). He considered that this progressive measure would be complete if sexual enlightenment was added to the child's store of knowledge.

It is noteworthy how much Klein's project with Eric was precisely this attempt to enlighten him sexually in order to awaken his healthy curiosity and establish a scientific, reality-orientated focus in his intellectual development. It also explains her great discomfort when Eric insisted on holding on to myths and religious symbols like the Easter Hare, Father Christmas, and angels. Ultimately, she had a very awkward confrontation with him over the existence of God. All this makes much more sense if her underlying beliefs about the importance for development of moving from omnipotence to reality are understood.

While this is an example of a direct influence, as I suggested, Ferenczi's influence was also complex and at times indirect. There was sometimes evidence of his influence even when their two outlooks bore little resemblance.

I will take as an example an element in their respective thinking on technique. In his paper "The elasticity in psychoanalytic technique", Ferenczi, characteristically, discusses the need for tact when interpreting to the patient. He sees tact as closely allied to empathy. He suggests that "The analyst, like an elastic band, must yield to the patient's pull, but without ceasing to pull in his own direction" (Ferenczi, 1928, p. 95). And he believes that tact, springing from empathy, is required in order to spare the patient overwhelming psychic pain. On the whole, tact was very much a hallmark of Ferenczi's nature. As someone highly aware of trauma, his type of tact and empathy were protective in essence, and he understood that interpretation can be traumatic.

Tact is not exactly the word that always springs to mind when thinking of Klein's mode of interpretation. She wanted her words to get to the heart of unconscious anxiety, and believed that delving directly into the unconscious would produce recognition and relief. Klein imagined that the patient's unconscious listens readily and responds so powerfully as to override all other factors. Tact has no role in this outlook. We see the difficulties that arose from this belief in her treatment of Richard, for example, where his discomfort with her interpretations, and his inability to profit from them are always in evidence at moments when she delves without restraint into his psyche.

But perhaps tact and tactlessness are also bound up with Klein's and Ferenczi's different views of intimacy. For Klein, intimacy amounted to unconscious recognition. The analyst was to provide psychic company where the patient needed it most—in his lonely stand against his own destructiveness and psychotic anxieties, whereas for Ferenczi, intimacy was empathy for the psychically defended subject, and a high awareness that interpretation, especially deep interpretation, can violate and traumatise. The patient is, thus, to be offered what he called "maternal friendliness". Ferenczi's analysand, Sandor Loránd noted how Ferenczi was highly aware of the significance of the patient's "bodily movements, positions, gesticulations, modulations of voice and the like" (Grosskurth, 1987). The patient's most intimate communication was to be noted by the analyst, but to be used in interpretation with the tact of maternal friendliness.

Yet, even this assumption is not straightforward. When faced with exasperating clinical situations, Ferenczi's tact was tested to a point that strained his technique. He inevitably came across patients who, in his words, "could not get beyond 'dead points' [dead point in Hungarian = being stuck] in analysis". From his description, some of these individuals sound as though they were suffering from a personality disorder, which is notoriously difficult for the analyst to endure. But even if this did not apply to all of them, Ferenczi discovered that it is precisely tact that is tested to the limit with some patients. In some situations, psychic progress was slow and deeply frustrating. Ferenczi's response was not to interpret destructive, deadly inertia, but to invent a technique that urged constructive, lively action—his active technique. Since clinical impasse presents the most difficult issue, it was legitimate to try out various techniques in order to explore possibilities. But Ferenczi's choice of experimental technique happens to have been the advocating of action, and this must have been at least partly an attempt to relieve the analyst from the tactless, unempathic experience of hate in the countertransference. Perhaps Klein even felt at times that he was avoiding necessary confrontations in her analysis, and she seems to have felt that he did not take up the negative transference. The result was her own technique, which addresses destructive tendencies directly.

The subject of technique does not end with this. It is surprising, for instance, to discover elements in Ferenczi's technique that closely resemble contemporary Kleinian thinking. As an example, I will take the idea of working in the here-and-now. In his 1925 monograph written jointly with Otto Rank, Ferenczi suggests that the point of analysis is not to prove the "correctness of theory". Rather, it "consists in understanding and interpreting every expression of the patient above all as a reaction to the present analytical situation (defence against, or recognition of the exposition of the analyst, emotional reactions to these, etc.) . . ." (Ferenczi & Rank, 1925).

In other words, this here-and-now interpretation was supposed not just to address the here-and-now, but also to comment on the use that the patient makes, or fails to make, of the analyst's thinking: as Ferenczi puts it, the "defence against, or recognition of" the analyst's comments. This is something that is still practised and has been developed, for example, by Betty Joseph. How has contemporary Kleinian thinking come to resemble so closely Ferenczi's ideas, given that he was largely ignored by Klein's followers until recently?

Perhaps this becomes less surprising when we consider that Klein herself did much work in the here-and-now, at least according to her published clinical vignettes. There is, thus, evidence for a theory of technique passed from Ferenczi via Klein into contemporary thinking. Of course, this move is not a simple passing on of a single idea. Klein's preference for the here-and-now resulted also from her view of the transference. In her thinking, it was specifically internal objects that were transferred on to the arena of analysis, and not so much people from the patient's past. The analysis, thus, had to address the patient's internal object relationships in the present, rather than focus on reminiscences of actual past relationships. But, in all likelihood, Klein experienced some here-and-now work with Ferenczi, and we can see the far-reaching consequences of this.

There is another thought that arises from this. The content of some here-and-now interpretations can be anything but tactful, especially if they point out what Ferenczi described as the patient's "defence against" the analyst's words. We do not know how Ferenczi handled this. But the implications of his theory are there: that the analytic stance is one of tact and empathy, and, therefore, that a punitive style is to be avoided when destructive material is addressed.

References

Ferenczi, S. (1908). Psycho-analysis and education. In: *Final Contributions to the Problems and Methods of Psycho-Analysis* (pp. 280–290), M. Balint (Ed.), E. Mosbacher & others (Trans.). London: Hogarth Press, 1955 [reprinted, London: Karnac, 1994].

Ferenczi, S. (1913). Stages in the development of the sense of reality. In: *First Contribution to Psycho-Analysis by Sándor Ferenczi* (pp. 213–239). London: Hogarth Press, 1952 [reprinted, London: Karnac, 1994].

Ferenczi, S. (1928). The elasticity of psychoanalytic technique. In: *Final Contributions to the Problems and Methods of Psycho-Analysis* (pp. 87–101), M. Balint (Ed.), E. Mosbacher & others (Trans.). London: Hogarth Press, 1955 [reprinted, London: Karnac, 1994].

Ferenczi, S., & Rank, O. (1925). *The Development of Psycho-Analytic Technique*. New York: International Universities Press, 1986.

Grosskurth, P. (1987). *Melanie Klein, Her World and Her Work*. Cambridge, MA: Harvard University Press.

Klein, M. (1921). The development of a child. In: *Love, Guilt and Reparation* (pp. 1–53). London: Hogarth Press, 1975.

Likierman, M. (2001). *Melanie Klein: Her Work in Context*. London: Continuum.

Petot, J.-M. (1990). *Melanie Klein, Volume 1: First Discoveries and First System 1919–1932*. Madison, CT: International Universities Press.

PART II

FROM FERENCZI TO
WINNICOTT AND DOLTO

CHAPTER THREE

Early emotional development: Ferenczi to Winnicott[1]

Margaret Tonnesmann

erenczi wrote his paper, "Stages in the development of the sense of reality" (Ferenczi, 1913) just two years after Freud had published his "Formulations on the two principles of psychic functioning" (Freud, 1911b), because he felt that Freud had not explained how the transition from the pleasure principle to the reality principle takes place during early infancy.

Ferenczi's paper acknowledges the classical instinct theory of the time: the reproductive libidinal instincts and self-preservative instincts, which, at that time, were called "ego-instincts". Ferenczi reasons that development from the pleasure principle to the reality principle is probably due to the replacement of childhood megalomania by the recognition of the power of natural forces, and that this constitutes the essential content of ego development. He draws attention to the famous footnote in Freud's paper, that an organisation that is a slave to the pleasure principle and that can neglect the reality of the external world is a fiction, but is almost realised provided one includes with it the care a child receives from its mother.

However, Ferenczi then points out that such an organisation is realised in the embryo's existence in the womb, as there is indeed total environmental supply and with it absolute omnipotence. There is no wish-impulse yet. When, during the post-uterine existence, this stage is, as Ferenczi put it, rudely interrupted, it is the loving and empathic nursing care that gratifies the first wish-impulses of the infant. In magic hallucinatory omnipotence, the infant can imagine satisfaction in positive and negative hallucinations.

As the infant's psychic organisation grows, what had been simple phenomenal discharge of unpleasant affects now obtains a new function and can be used to give signals, so that hallucinatory ideational identity can be followed by satisfying perceptual identity. Thus, the infant can maintain its omnipotence with the help of magic gestures, which, in time, become more and more complex and specialised. They all call for prompt satisfaction, which is given by the mother's loving attention and appropriate nursing care. But the infant experiences this as part of his self and he is not aware of mother's administrations to satisfy his needs. Ferenczi conceived of this earliest development as the introjective omnipotent stage, which, in time, gives way to the beginnings of the projective reality stage of the ego. The infant now experiences—often painfully—that the outside world does not always obey his magic gestures, and instant gratification of his wishes and wants might be delayed or absent. In a further advance of adaptation, the ego starts to distinguish between subjective psychical contents, that is to say, his feelings, and the objective content of sensations. The outside world, however, is at first endowed with life by the infant during the animistic period of development. In the reality-objects, he seeks his own body organs and activities, which is the beginning of symbol formation. He also learns to represent the outside world symbolically by means of his own body. Ferenczi is aware here of the importance of the environmental provisions when he states that the understanding, loving care the infant receives from his mother is the reason it need not give up the illusion of omnipotence as yet.

In time, the baby starts to make use of speech symbolism, beginning with the imitation of sounds and noises. He discovers that this allows for a much simpler and more varied representation of objects in the outside world than was possible with gesture language. In further development, conscious thinking makes speech symbolism possible by association with thought processes that are in themselves unconscious, lending them perceptual qualities. This is the development of conscious thought that advances the ego's adjustment to reality, as Freud had already said, but it is the continuation of mother's care that, by guessing the child's thoughts, allows him an additional period when he can experience his own thoughts and words as having magic power. Referring to Freud, Ferenczi agreed that it is only with the child's psychical detachment from his parents that the feelings of omnipotence give way to full appreciation of the force of circumstances.

What seems remarkable about this paper is that it represents (in 1913!) a highly intuitive and detailed study of ego development in infancy and it also recognises the importance of mother's adaptations to her infant's needs for the undisturbed continuation of his maturational omnipotence. It is a paper of classical orientation, and it essentially views development as a series of internal adaptations. It conceives of the infant in terms of a one-body psychology, to use Rickman's classification of a one-, two-, three- and multi-body psychology.

What might also be of interest is that, in this paper, Ferenczi talks tentatively of the idea that in psycho-neurotic pathology not only is there regression to fixation points of libidinal development, but, in primary repression, a developmentally corresponding part of mental functioning is also arrested, and does not take part in further development with the rest of the ego. He reasons that the mechanisms of neurotic symptoms are determined by regression to this early arrested ego part. Hysteria, for example, is characterised, on the one hand, by regression to early libidinal fixations, and, on the other hand, by regression to the corresponding arrested fixations of the ego, that is to say, to the stage of magic gestures that characterises conversion. In obsessional neurosis there is also regression to an arrested ego part at the stage of magic omnipotent thought.

In the introduction to her first book, *Psycho-analysis of Children*, Klein (1932) expressed her indebtedness to her two teachers: Sandor Ferenczi and Karl Abraham. She explicitly states that apart from his strong and immediate feelings for the unconscious and symbolism, Ferenczi impressed her by his unusual empathy for the psyche of the small child. She also says that she owes to Ferenczi the foundation of her personal development as a psychoanalyst. She characterised Abraham as her mentor, and deeply appreciated his highest expectations of the human and scientific achievements of his colleagues, which she said had inspired her. By the time she came to England in 1926, she had had analysis with Ferenczi, whose capacity for emotional understanding and relating to children she had admired, and she had also had analysis with Abraham, whose late work concerned the fate of the libidinal object in development and pathology. As she herself has acknowledged, both analysts were important for the development of her own theories of child development.

Her ideas on early object relations stimulated discussion in the British Society, where there had already been great interest in early development of affects by analysts such as Ernest Jones, Edward Glover, and others. In her classical paper on affects, Brierley (1937) gave high priority to effect-cathexis from the beginning, and said that initially the effect is the object for the infant. It is the cathexis of the object, rather than the emotional charge of the ideational representation of the impulse, that is central to all the various object-relations theories.

Melanie Klein developed her theories of early object-relations while remaining committed to instinct theory. Her concepts assume instinctual conflicts with objects manifested in unconscious phantasies, and activating the primitive defence mechanisms of an operative primitive ego from birth. Hence, her theories of object-relations are also of a one-body-psychology order. Supported by the loving care of the nursing mother, the developmental processes unfold according to the infant's constitutional forces, which built the structure of the child's internal object world.

It was different for those British analysts of an object-relations theoretical orientation, foremost of them Balint, Fairbairn, and Winnicott, but also many others, who conceived of object-relations not primarily as cathexis of the object of the instinctual impulses, but as an intersubjective emotional process operative from the earliest dependence of the infant on the nursing mother. She it is who contributes the fateful facilitating environment for the infant's maturational processes. This is a two-body psychology.

Fairbairn (1946) stated that from the word go the ego is not pleasure-seeking, but object-seeking, and Balint was at pains to insist that there is no primary narcissism, but secondary narcissism from the beginning—the narcissistic solution to early object-relating.

Winnicott conceived of earliest development as a mother–infant unity. He coined the phrase "I cannot conceive of an infant, only of a nursing couple". His main concern was the study of ego-relatedness, that is, object-relating apart from id considerations. Contrary to Fairbairn's view, he did not give up instinct theory altogether, but stressed that instinctual impulses are an important back-up for ego relatedness.

Winnicott felt that psychoanalysis had concentrated its attention on psychic reality and shared reality, but neglected the intermediate area of experience, which is neither intrapsychic nor shared reality, but is at the border of the two, with both contributing to it. This third area, in Winnicott's concept of infant development, is a potential space; he places the experiential, emotional quality of the infant–mother unity at the centre of his considerations (Winnicott, 1971). He conceived of an infant at the very beginning in absolute or double dependence on the nursing mother. The infant is dependent, but has no awareness of it yet. The ordinary devoted mother relates to the infant with what he called maternal preoccupation, which is given to her in health, prepared during the last stages of pregnancy,

Donald Winnicott, by Olga Székely-Kovacs.

and lasts for a couple of months. At the beginning, she holds the infant's ego so is aware of her infant's needs. At first the infant has only motor sensory experiences and is totally merged with the mother in a state of anxiety-free unintegration, a kind of continuation of the intrauterine existence, where physiology and psychology are not yet differentiated and the environmental provision assures life of the tissue. Ferenczi describes the nursing care of the post-uterine infant in similar terms, but for him it is not the mother's loving administrations of keeping her infant warm and protected from noise and light that approximate the infant's wish to go back into the wishless intrauterine state where everything was provided for. Winnicott maintained that the ordinary devoted mother meets the infant's needs by empathically understanding what the infant is feeling. She makes sure that his experience of continuity-of-going-on-being is not interrupted. Winnicott demarcates from it the mother–infant relationship built on satisfaction of instinctual impulses.

The mother also facilitates experientially creating the object by the infant. The infant has a wish, a want for the breast, and at this moment the mother presents the breast to the infant. Omnipotently, the infant experiences that he has created an object, the breast, just when it was wanted. Here, the hallucination is a creative gesture. This is akin to Ferenczi's stage of hallucinatory magic omnipotence, when perceptual identity follows the ideational one, but, for Winnicott, it is the experience that leaves memory traces of a special kind. If, however, the mother is insensitive to the infant's needs and presents, let us say, the nipple in an unsatisfactory position, the infant's feelings of continuity-of-being are impinged upon and, whereas in good-enough mothering the infant can gather such occasional failures under his omnipotence, frequent crises of a not-good-enough mother lead to early dissociation. The self withdraws from communication and instead a compliant, false self develops, accompanied by premature mind activity. Spontaneous affect signals disappear and, instead, the infant only reacts compliantly and, therefore, defensively to stimuli. Winnicott assumes that this very early split protects the true self from further impingements, but it also prevents its further growth and can lead to severe pathology of childhood psychosis and autism. For Ferenczi, it is regression to arrested parts at the stage of magic hallucinatory wish-fulfilment that constitutes the mechanism of psychotic symptoms.

According to Ferenczi's one-body psychology approach, ego development in early infancy is due to the adaptation to increasing frustration of the infant's omnipotent wishes and wants. In the course of development, the infant experiences that not all urges find instant magic satisfaction, and it slowly dawns on him that there are hostile forces in the outside world, when, for example, an object he stretches his arms out for does not come to him. It is from the experience of this painful discordance that the ego learns to differentiate between the outer world and its psychic feeling world. In other words, the infant perceives the separateness of objects through frustration of its omnipotent wishes.

Winnicott's approach is of a two-body psychology. He conceptualises this developmental step differently: when ego relatedness has become possible, there develops a space between mother and infant. It is the area of illusion, in which the infant's subjective relating is imaginatively and experientially enriched. He refers to the observation that infants early on, when vigorously sucking the breast, might simultaneously stroke their lips with a finger or caress the breast with their hand. Libidinal and aggressive impulses are still unintegrated and the infant might experience them as coming from outside. For the infant, he says, the impulse is just like a clap of thunder. In a primitive love impulse, the infant might wish to destroy his subjective object joyfully and—as Winnicott says—give it cavalier-fashion treatment, but there is no malice in this: "I love you, so I eat you". Here, the good-enough mother will understand the importance of her survival of the attack. It is one of the most important developmental steps, as the infant's discovery of the survival of the destroyed object releases it from his omnipotent control. The infant can relate to a separate object. In Winnicott's concept, it is not the absence of gratification that introduces the infant to shared reality and with it a separate object world; it is the survival of the object he has destroyed in subjective intention that matters. Now it can be trusted and used. The healthy infant has now reached the status of a unit with boundaries, and ego relating is enhanced by the triad of introjection, projection, and identification. Aggressive and libidinal impulses become fused and, in time, the self will take responsibility for them. It is only then that we can speak of a hateful destructive impulse and also of developing concern for the separate object and its intrapsychic imago.

It seems to me that it is here, in the different assumptions about the infant's learning of an adapting to shared reality, that the contrast between Ferenczi's one-body psychology and Winnicott's two-body psychology is most striking. In a second paper (Ferenczi, 1926), which is influenced by Freud's final instinct theory, Ferenczi further discussed development towards the reality principle. He stressed there that as long as the infant is in the stage of introjective omnipotent development, he has no feelings for the object, neither good ones nor bad. As long as the object is always there when needed, it is experienced as part of the ego. But when the object remains absent when needed, and that is, for example, when the infant feels hungry but there is no breast, we can observe that the infant reacts with uncoordinated movements and screaming, comparable with an adult's expression of rage. Ferenczi reasons that a de-fusion of instincts takes place here and the destructive part takes prevalence. The absent object is now hated. When, however, the object reappears and the infant finds it again, the libidinal part takes over and the refound object can now be loved. This is in line with Freud's statement that all object finding is a refinding of it. It is from the first experience of the absence of the object that is needed, or, as Ferenczi said in 1913, when the infant discovers that not everything obeys his will, that the infant is introduced to the notion of reality-objects, which are then ambivalently hated when absent, but loved when refound.

Winnicott's assumptions are different, as he did not accept the concept of the death instinct. He traced the roots of aggression to prenatal life and saw in the muscular movements that meet opposition the earliest manifestations of pleasurable aggression. At the beginning, these movements are physiological me/not-me pre-experiences. The aggressive impulse is purposeful, but in subjective omnipotence the infant does not know about it: he is pre-ruth rather than ruthless, as Winnicott said. Only after the object has been released from the infant's omnipotent control can he experience hate towards the—now separate—object.

As I have already said, in further development, Ferenczi assumes an animistic phase when the infant endows objects of the outer world with life and seeks to find again in his objects his own body organs and their pleasurable activities. It is the stage of the beginnings of symbol formation, enriched by imitation, imagination, and experimentation. In time, the child develops speech, and conscious thinking makes speech symbolism possible by becoming associated with unconscious thought processes.

Winnicott emphasised that in further emotional development it is the child's dependence on the mother, who is now experienced as a separate object and, in health, a trustworthy one, that is important. The mother continues to provide understanding ego cover appropriate to the maturational age of her child. She will now start to disillusion the infant, let it wait for a bit, etc., and whereas impingement during earliest development leads to catastrophic pathology, as I have already stated, it now assumes positive value, as it stimulates the infant's capacity to communicate. Instead of elaborating the animistic stage of development, as Ferenczi had done, Winnicott's interest was in exploring further emotional development in the third area of experience. His concepts of the transitional object and transitional phenomena are central to an understanding of the vital position he gives to ego relatedness and the development of the individual's interactional emotional relating. The first object of which the child takes possession and which is neither a projection of an internal object nor a shared reality-object, though both contribute to it, remains in the experiential space. It has to have features of both the self and the mother, and it has to have all the characteristics of surviving when used. It should be indestructible and remain the same however it is maltreated at times by the baby's vigorous love and hate.

Winnicott accepts that the transitional object is at the root of symbol development and represents the infant–mother unity, but he stressed that, for him, it is the use the infant makes of his transitional object that is important. It covers the whole range of the emotional experiences of the self. When, with further development, the transitional object is forgotten, as the baby's interests widen into the area of transitional phenomena, (the child's self-absorbed playing) and later to cultural experiences in the widest sense of the term, they cover everything that we say is meaningful to us. The core self, or true self, as Winnicott called it to contrast it with his concept of the false self, remains, in his assumption, an isolate and is incommunicable. But it actualises itself in the transitional space that he called the third area of experience. Winnicott maintained that the child's playing is a capacity that remains active in all healthy-enough human beings throughout life. Playing is doing, he said, and he differentiated it sharply from narcissistic libidinal daydreaming. He also drew attention to the fact that id excitement, when it reaches a certain threshold, interrupts the child's playing. Playing was, for him, not just mastery of trauma; neither was it only sublimation of instinctual impulses. What matters in playing is the self's actualisation and the creativity of ego relatedness. It is from these assumptions, he said, that all meaningful relationships between human beings, and also the psychoanalytic therapy process, take place, in a space to which both partners contribute and where two areas of playing overlap. In adult analysis, he said, playing manifests itself, for example, in the choice of words, in the intonation of voice, and also in the sense of humour.

I have tried to compare and to contrast two psychoanalytic theories of infant development. Ferenczi's paper of 1913 must be the first, or one of the first, papers on baby observation. The infant's development is viewed in terms of the classical theory of the time: the ego's adaptation to the demands of shared reality with the aim finding satisfaction for the tension states that are caused by the growing infant's ever increasing wishes and wants. Ferenczi views the infant in terms of a one-body psychology, but he also describes mother's nursing care at different stages, so that the infant can live with appropriate feelings of omnipotence and the formation of pathogenic fixations, and arrests can be minimised.

Winnicott's object-relations theory of infant development is a two-body psychology. He views development as evolving from the infant–mother unity with its interactional emotional dependence. The unfolding of emotional experiences in ego relatedness and the actualisation of self in creative pursuits are, for him, the base of healthy development. Pathology might arise when, owing to extensive failures of the nursing mother, the infant's continuity-of-being feelings are repeatedly impinged upon. An endopsychic defensive adaptation to shared reality develops in a false-self organisation with premature mind activity. During the 1920s, Ferenczi treated some severely disturbed patients, and difficulties arose when these patients experienced his classical, benevolent, neutral, analytic stance as being cold, harsh, or aloof towards them. To bring the analytic process forward, he relaxed his attitude and encouraged the patients' tendencies to regress during the sessions. They then re-enacted, in a trance-like state, childhood memories, and Ferenczi responded by trying to address in them the child that they had become at such moments. When, after a while, he brought such episodes to a close and addressed the adult patient again, the patients reacted with vehement anger, and Ferenczi became aware that the patients had first regressed to a pre-trauma stage, but, with his change of approach, had re-experienced a childhood trauma that they could now recall in memory. This led him to investigate the exogenous factors in infant and child development, in particular those traumatic events in the infant– and child–mother relationship that were of pathogenic significance.

His theoretical orientation had now shifted from a one-body psychology to a two-body one. He felt that it was rather naïve of him to rediscover what he had, after all, known but neglected for twenty-five years. At the 1929 International Congress in Oxford, he said that however half-worked-out his theoretical statements were, he was convinced that a proper evaluation of the long neglected traumatogenesis was necessary for our practical technique and the theory of our science.

It is with the evaluation of pathogenic early traumata that Ferenczi's and Winnicott's concepts, to some extent, converge, as both held the same basic assumptions: that the mother–infant and mother–child interactions are of vital importance for the emotional and mental health of the individual. Both authors assume that privation and deprivation, to use Winnicott's terminology, lead to narcissistic splits of the self and only by re-experiencing such early traumata during analysis can these splits be healed.

When traumata have occurred before the infant has reached unit status, in Winnicott's formulation, or, in Ferenczi's words, before the infant has reached the stage of development when thought has completely developed, they are only registered in physical memories. Winnicott called them frozen memories and stressed that they often accurately resemble the original trauma. Ferenczi stated that such memories could only be repeated in transitory hysterical symptoms that signify regression to the stage of magic gestures. In the analytic situation, they have communicative emotional value in the analyst–patient relationship. Winnicott has stressed that such severely regressed patients need management rather than interpretation, and the analyst has to provide "holding" for the vulnerable, dependent patient. Ferenczi also said that such patients, who often present with a loss of desire for life, feelings of having been abandoned, and who also show signs of having turned the aggression against the self, need a period of indulgence preparatory to later analysis.

Ferenczi's main interest, however, was with those infantile trau- mata that the patients could recall in memory. He conceived the trau- matogenic factor as the mother's, or, in cases of the child's sexual or violent abuse, the adult's failure to respond to the child's innocent, guilt-free, tender feelings and phantasies of passive love. Instead, the other reacts with feelings of love and hate that belong to the adult's passionate emotions, and they are often consciously denied. The child now feels not understood, abandoned, not confirmed in the reality of his own emotional state, and he becomes confused and frightened. He instantly identifies with the aggressor, leading to a split in the self and endopsychic manifestations that are similar to those described by Winnicott as false-living in cases of false-self development. Ferenczi attempted to find a technique that would not only repeat the trauma, but also allow the patient to experience in the analytic relationship the analyst as a new object who responds with complete frankness about his own feelings when the patient experiences him in the transference as the aggressor. These were early attempts to accommodate counter- transference for the benefit of the patient.

Winnicott's concept is different. He conceived of false-self disor- ders as defences to protect the true or core self from traumatic envi- ronmental intrusions. Another category of response to traumata is the antisocial tendency of a child that feels it has the right to take back what it once had, but was taken away from him (mother's love) when a sibling is born, for example, or when sometimes, owing to external circumstances, she has to withdraw some of her attention. Stealing and lying are characteristic features of the antisocial tendency and, when not given attention, can result in massive character disorders with secondary gains. Winnicott was sceptical about the value of psychoanalytic treatment in such cases.

Sandor Ferenczi died at the age of sixty, and with it his research into the traumatogenic origin of self-disorders and his search for a technique that could utilise countertransference in the best interest of the patients came to a premature end. On several occasions, he made a plea in his last papers for a more thorough analysis of practising psychoanalysts, and he expressed concern that otherwise a situation could arise when patients had become better analysed than their analysts. Fifteen years later, Winnicott can take training analysis for granted when he requires that the analyst has to understand his own guilt about his primitive unconscious destructive impulses during treating patients who suffer from narcissistic depressions and who need the analyst to survive, and, also, when treating psychotic patients, the analyst has to be able to experience and to contain his undisplaced simultaneous love and hate in countertransference.

Ferenczi was always somewhat ahead of his time. That was already so when, in 1913, he wrote his fine paper on baby observation, focusing on early development in terms of the various stages that lead finally to the baby's adaptation to reality. As I have already said, he stated there that primal repression is accompanied by a corresponding arrest of parts of the ego. In Fairbairn's two-body object-relations theory, object–ego relationships are split, repressed, and constitute psychic structure. In his late papers, Ferenczi discussed theory and technique of self-disorders resulting from infantile pathogenic traumata. This was also ahead of his time, as the understanding of the communicative value of emotions in an intersubjective transference–countertransference relationship was neither comprehended nor practised in 1933. If he could have survived for another fifteen years or so, would he have developed his traumatogenic theory in similar directions to those of Balint or Winnicott, or even Fairbairn? Would he have come to conclusions similar to Heimann's in 1950, or Winnicott's in 1947, or King's in 1978 concerning the handling of the counter-transference in psychoanalytic therapy?

In the context of *Ferenczi for Our Time*, I have tried to trace in Ferenczi's contributions to psychoanalyses the development from a one-body to a two-body psychology, which foreshadowed those object-relations theories that Winnicott and other British psychoanalysts have developed and that are practised in particular by analysts of the Independent Group of psychoanalysis in the UK.

Note

1. Editors' note: The references might not be complete due to the fact that in the past few years Margaret Tonnesmann has unfortunately not been able to participate in our pre-publication consultations any longer.

References

Brierley, M. (1937). Affects in theory and practice. *International Journal of Psychoanalysis, 18*: 256–268.

Fairbairn, W. D. (1946). Object relationships and dynamic structure. *International Journal of Psychoanalysis*, 27: 30–37.

Ferenczi, S. (1913). Stages in the development of the sense of reality. In: *First Contributions to the Problems and Methods of Psycho-Analysis*. London: Maresfield Reprints, 1952.

Ferenczi, S. (1926). The problem of the acceptance of unpleasant ideas-advances in knowledge of the sense of reality. In: *Further Contributions to the Theory and Technique of Psycho-Analysis* (pp. 7–9), J. Rickman (Ed.), J. I. Suttie and others (Trans.). London: Hogarth Press, 1955.

Freud, S. (1911b). Formulations on the two principles of psychic functioning. *S.E., 12*: 218–226.

Heimann, P. (1950). On counter-transference. *International Journal of Psychoanalysis, 31*: 81–84.

King, P. (1978). Affective response of the analyst to the patient's communication. *International Journal of Psychoanalysis, 59*: 329–334.

Klein, M. (1932). *The Psycho-Analysis of Children*. London: International Psycho-Analytical Library, Hogarth Press.

Winnicott, D. W. (1949). Hate in the counter-transference. *International Journal of Psychoanalysis, 30*: 69–74.

Winnicott, D. W. (1971). *Playing and Reality*. London: Tavistock.

CHAPTER FOUR

"Thalassa to the ocean": from Sandor Ferenczi to Françoise Dolto

Kathleen Kelley-Lainé

Freud's "Oceanic feeling", Ferenczi's "Thalassa", and Dolto's "Wave and the ocean" all take us back to the question of our origins, when we felt "one" with our environment, before even the word "mother" existed, because it was not necessary. Before language, before separation, before conflict—is this the place of returning that forever fascinates us, engenders our curiosity, and from where all theories arise?

Sandor Ferenczi and Françoise Dolto, perhaps more than others, based their clinical work, as well as their conceptualisation of psychoanalysis, on the fundamental enigma of human existence: "where babies come from and where the dead go". Ferenczi and Dolto were creative innovators who were admired by their colleagues, but marginalised institutionally in official psychoanalytical circles for what were considered to be unorthodox thinking and methods. Ferenczi's ground-breaking work on "counter-transference" and the importance of the person of the analyst, might have threatened Freud's attempts to establish psychoanalysis as a science. He actively opposed Ferenczi's presentation of "The confusion of tongues", a paper that seemingly attacked Freud's cold and rigid attitude to patients. Dolto's innovative conception of the child as a "person" to be spoken to and treated as a human being from before birth was certainly revolutionary in a society whose word for child (*enfant*) means "he who does not speak". Her exceptional success in the treatment of psychotic children through her particular use of language was highly appreciated by some and became the subject of strong suspicion by others.

What do Sandor Ferenczi, a Hungarian Jew, and Françoise Dolto, a French Catholic, have in common? Despite the significant differences between them, Françoise Dolto and Sandor Ferenczi share a number of biographical as well as psychological elements. Both were born into large families with numerous children—Françoise Marette, born in Paris in 1908, was the fourth child in a family of seven. Sandor Ferenczi, born in Hungary in 1873, was the seventh of twelve children. Although the Marette family was part of the *grand bourgeoisie* in a French Catholic milieu, Françoise's maternal grandfather, Arthur Demmler, had been a poor immigrant from Germany. Ferenczi's father had come from Poland to escape the pogroms. Both immigrant branches were quickly integrated into the main culture through hard work and exceptional skills. Françoise's grandfather Demmler graduated from l'Ecole Polytechnique, one of the most prestigious institutes of higher education in France and one that ensures upward mobility.

Ferenczi's father, who, at the age of eighteen, fought for Hungarian liberation in the revolution of 1848–1849, worked his way up from shop assistant to owner of a bookstore in Miskolc that was to become an important cultural centre in the city, a meeting place for artists, musicians, and writers. Soon, the Ferenczis were into the publishing business and contributing to the cultural progress of Hungary. Both families shared the dynamics of upward social mobility. How did this affect the children?

Sibling rivalry, immigration, integration, and early encounters with death are some of the common elements in the biographies of Ferenczi and Dolto. Sandor's father died when he was only fifteen years old. He had been a favourite son and his father's death was a serious trauma in his life: he was left with a strict and intolerant mother, who did not provide him with the love and tenderness that he craved. In 1923, he wrote a paper entitled "The dream of the wise baby", in which he identified a phenomenon he had discovered through his clinical work: young children who had been traumatised often had accelerated developmental characteristics which resulted in their having highly acute sensitivities and intuitions—in short, wisdom beyond their years. Was Ferenczi himself this wise baby?

Françoise Dolto was twelve years old when her older sister Jacqueline died of cancer at the age of sixteen. Jacqueline had been her mother's favourite daughter, as she was the only one to have inherited Arthur Demmler's blue eyes. She was already very ill when Françoise was to be confirmed into the church, and her mother told her that children who pray to God with an innocent heart are able to save the dying. Françoise prayed but her sister died; her mother never forgave her, blaming her for the death of Jacqueline. Françoise had already decided to become a *medecin* d'education (doctor of education) to save children and their parents from grave misunderstandings and miscommunication.

In an autobiographical interview, Dolto recounts that at age four she was passionately interested in knowing what happens after death, and asked her nanny where dead people go:

> She (the nanny) became quiet for a time and looked very serious and troubled. I said, 'But this time I really want to know' and I latched onto her arm, jumping up and down . . . I remember very well. Then

Françoise Dolto.

she said, 'But you know, Vava, they bury the body and the soul goes to heaven.' 'To heaven, to heaven, what is that, and what's it like?' 'Well, they say . . .' she said. 'But in fact you don't know?' I asked. Then she said, 'No, I don't know. They believe, but no one knows.' Then, apparently, (she told me this afterwards) I didn't say another word during the walk and when we arrived home I went to the window; there was always death and the window . . . why death and the window? Because the window (*fenêtre, la première fait-naître, voir la lumière, c'est la mort du foetus, pour que le bébé ait la vie*) it is something to do with the meaning of giving light, to be or not to be. (Dolto, 1986, p. 12)

She stayed by the window for two days, thinking about death, the fact that adults continued to go about their lives even though they did not have the answer to where babies come from and where the dead go. She said that from then on she felt sorry for adults, as if they were no more powerful than children, since they were just as ignorant about the fundamental questions of life.

Despite many hardships with her mother, who did not want her to be educated, let alone become a doctor, Françoise Dolto studied to be a paediatrician. She later trained as a psychoanalyst and was a collaborator of Lacan. Not only was she renowned for her work as a child analyst, she was also the first to popularise psychoanalysis via the media. In the 1970s, she had a regular radio programme to which the public could send their written questions and she would discuss these openly with the listeners. She educated France in child psychology.

Sandor spent his childhood browsing among the shelves of the bookstore that his mother took over after the untimely death of her husband. His vivid curiosity led him to read and cultivate himself in the arts, literature, and music. This might also have been his way to try to compensate for the love he did not receive from his emotionally distant mother. He recorded his memories of this emotional lack in his clinical diaries, written in 1932, and he is probably writing about himself in his work entitled "The unwanted child and the death instinct" (Ferenczi, 1929, p. 102). He studied medicine in Vienna at the age of seventeen and then practised as a neurologist in Budapest. He was introduced to Freud's writings by a friend and met Freud in 1908, when their friendship, correspondence, and analytical relationship began.

During their psychoanalytical careers, both Dolto and Ferenczi came to be marginalised as unorthodox by the mainstream analytical society. Ferenczi's privileged position with Freud lasted until he began questioning the master's ideas, especially those concerning analytical techniques and methods. In 1989, Ferenczi published *Thalassa: A Theory of Genitality*. It was in these years that Ferenczi made a name for himself as someone willing to take on cases that appeared to be utterly hopeless; it was against this backdrop that he began his technical innovations. Although some of these innovations were substantiated in the light of later practice, from the start of the 1920s they resulted in a serious difference of opinion between him and Freud. Ferenczi radicalised psychoanalysis with the insight that the therapeutic act itself—the hypocritical conduct of the therapist remaining aloof from the patient—is, in fact, a repetition of the patient's childhood trauma.

Freud was concerned that Ferenczi might compromise psychoanalysis with the "therapy of indulgence". It must have been even harder for him to digest Ferenczi's paper "The confusion of tongues" (Ferenczi, 1955, p. 156), wherein he reconsidered the theory of seduction as a real trauma instead of phantasy, despite Freud's abandonment of his initial seduction theory.

It was in the course of therapeutic practice that the idea of mutual analysis arose, an idea also resented in professional circles. Although Ferenczi refused to apply this method later on, mutual analysis highlighted the fact that complete neutrality in therapy cannot be sustained, and that a defining component of the therapeutic process is the personality of the therapist himself. Ferenczi was the first to report on countertransference as an essential part of therapy; this phenomenon had been regarded as a disturbing by-product of psychoanalysis. It was experience gained from mutual analysis that alerted experts to the fact that a therapist must have a high degree of self-knowledge, which is best acquired by subjecting oneself to training-orientated psychoanalysis under the assumption that "the best therapist is a healed patient".

Perhaps the most sensitive aspect of the *Clinical Diary* (Ferenczi, 1932) is that, while criticising psychoanalysis, Ferenczi also criticises his own analysis, and, at the same time, that of his mentor, Freud. Ferenczi's main point of criticism against Freud was the inflexibility and remoteness with which he treated his patients, and the fact that he "trained" his patients almost as though he were their teacher. Freud's criticism of his *furore sanandi* (passion to heal) was painful to Ferenczi, both as therapist and patient.

At the end of the *Diary*, Ferenczi emphasises a tragic dilemma: "Is the only possibility of my continued existence the renunciation of the largest part of one's own self, in order to carry out the will of that higher power to the end (as though it were my own)?" (1932, p. 212).

Ferenczi died of chronic leukaemia in April 1933. After his death, malicious rumours began to circulate alleging that Ferenczi, in the last years of his life, had become a psychiatric patient, and that it had been under the influence of illness that he had formulated his technical and theoretical innovations. Jones, jealous of his one-time analyst, Ferenczi, who, of all analysts, had perhaps been the closest to Freud, played a particularly prominent role in spreading such rumours. It is interesting to see how, years later, Françoise Dolto came to be criticised for similar "unorthodoxies", such as openness and innovative methods concerning the person of the analyst.

Despite her early determination to become a "doctor of education", Françoise Dolto waited until she was twenty-five to begin her medical studies; she had promised her mother not to study because it was believed that educated women would never marry. Her increasing unhappiness brought her into analysis in 1932 with René Laforgue, the president of the Paris Psychoanalytical Society. Her analysis freed her from bondage to her mother, and she succeeded in entering medical school. Shortly after finishing her medical studies on the relationship between psychoanalysis and paediatric medicine, she married a young Russian emigrant doctor, Boris Dolto.

In 1938, she discovered the work of Jacques Lacan and, like Ferenczi with Freud, she became his close collaborator. She criticised him from the outset, telling him that she could not understand his language: "I don't understand what you write". It is said that Lacan's answer was: "I try to write what you do in practice!" (Dolto, 1989). After the Second World War, Dolto found herself in the midst of the ongoing conflict in the Paris Psychoanalytical Society (SPP), of which she had become a full member. She was now part of the second generation of analysts who had undergone training; they would be training future candidates. There was considerable debate about training methods. Sacha Nacht, president at the time, wanted analytic education to provide greater discipline and medical authority. Some of the younger students were unhappy with his methods, finding them rigid and authoritarian. Dolto, together with Lacan, supported the students who were against Nacht's methods. By 1953, Lacan's objections to the training model, as well as his controversial practice of engaging in short psychoanalytical sessions, precipitated a split in the already divided Society. In June, Lacan left the SPP to found a new organisation, the French Psychoanalytical Society, and Dolto was among those on his side.

In 1955, at the Nineteenth Congress of the IPA, the president, Heinz Hartmann, announced that the committee set up to study the dissident group had recommended that it be excluded from membership in the IPA because of its "insufficient training facilities".

By 1963, after many negotiations, the group was offered the sanction of the IPA, but the price was to be the exclusion of Lacan and Dolto. Lacan was chastised for his short sessions, for having too many students, and for his unorthodox teaching. As for Dolto, Donald Winnicott claimed that her ideas about treating psychotic children were thirty years ahead of the field. But, at the same time, he insisted that she had too much intuition and not enough method to be a training analyst. A charge that had been made against Lacan was also used as an accusation against Dolto: her students were said to be in an uncontrolled positive transference towards her.

The IPA's demands tore apart the French Psychoanalytical Society. In a vote in November 1963, a majority of its members declared themselves willing to sacrifice Lacan and Dolto in order to receive the IPA's recognition. The vote split the Society in two: those who were willing to renounce Lacan and Dolto were accepted into the establishment, and the others joined Lacan and Dolto in a new group, the Freudian School of Paris.

Dolto was loyal to Lacan for another fifteen years, but their relationship began to fray as the School was increasingly dominated by Lacan's son-in-law, Jacques-Alain Miller, as well as by Lacan's new passion for systemising psychoanalytical texts mathematically. By 1978, Dolto had spoken openly about the School's problems and became a symbol of resistance for many Freudian School analysts. In January 1980, Lacan, already seriously ill with cancer, decided to dissolve the Freudian School. Lacan felt that as he had created the School, he had every right to disband it. Dolto led the analysts who felt that the School was a public institution to which they had contributed and it was not for Lacan to destroy. The irony of this final battle was that Dolto defended what she and Lacan had fought for in the beginning: the analyst's right to free expression, to disagree with established authority, and to participate in an open psychoanalytical society. To many of the Lacanians, it was now Dolto rather than Lacan who was trying to keep alive what had been most radical in Lacanian psychoanalytical politics.

It would seem that Dolto and Ferenczi were both highly appreciated for their innovative and creative contribution to psychoanalysis, while at the same time were ultimately marginalised for those very reasons. Neither Dolto nor Ferenczi was out to create a following, or an all-encompassing theory of psychoanalysis. For both, the roots of their theoretical reflections were from clinical practice, early childhood, and the mother–child relationship. Both were highly interested in the role of language and empathy in clinical practice. Both analysts insisted on the importance of the body in the psychoanalytical process.

I will now return to my title, "Thalassa and the ocean", and attempt the impossible by trying to provide a glimpse of Dolto's concept of the "death instinct"; it so motivated her childhood curiosity that it plunged her into a "schizoid" state, as she told her daughter in an interview years later (Dolto, 1986). Her "metaphor" for the death instinct is "the wave and the ocean"; just as for Ferenczi sexuality takes on the image of "thalassa".

To understand Dolto is not easy; her language is very personal, and she uses images and metaphors that one finds in the language of children. I suspect that it is precisely because she was able to keep her "primary child's tongue" that she was so successful in her therapy with children. When one reads her medical thesis, *Psychoanalyse et pédiatrie*, there is no denial of the fact that she is a Freudian and that her ideas emerge from orthodox psychoanalytical theories. However, most of what she wrote and taught was not about theory, but, rather, about her clinical practice; this was inspired by her notion of "unconscious image of the body", which is also present in her conception of the "death instinct", that is, the wave and the ocean.

According to Dolto, desiring tires us out, but we recuperate our strength through the "death instinct" which enables us to return to our basic image (of the body), to our fundamental narcissism, at moments of ultimate pleasure, such as orgasm, when the subject abandons himself. This idea is developed in her work on "The unconscious body image" (Dolto 1984), where she insists on the necessity of distinguishing the death instinct from aggressiveness, which belongs to the life instinct. She attributes the death instinct to resting, or sleep, when the body becomes "anonymous" and takes a rest from the subject's insistent desires. Dolto uses the metaphor of the "wave and the ocean", wherein the life and death instincts coincide as in coitus. The "wave" represents the individual at the maximum of his creativity or expression; after having reached the very top of his strength, he sinks into the undifferentiated ocean. This image symbolises the accomplishments of human genitality: always being pushed beyond itself, once the desire has been achieved, either in coitus or in a work of art, once the subject has given all he can, he may return to resting, sleeping, just as at the end of a life filled with struggling against the pull of the ocean, one can let go at last and find rest in death. This alternating movement between the wave and the ocean exemplifies the principle of homeostasis; the symbolic function merges with the biological at the genital stage, the ultimate level of humanisation. This is made possible through symbolic castration. The concept of "symbolic castration" is a fundamental principle of psychic growth for Françoise Dolto. She explains this in her book on the "Unconscious Body Image" (1984). The psychoanalytical meaning of the word "castration", unlike the literal meaning (i.e., the mutilation of the sex glands), describes the process by which a human being is made to understand, by another human being, that his way of accomplishing his desire is forbidden by law. This is signified through language, by gestures, mime, or words.

Dolto illustrates this with the metaphor of the individual as a plant. The plant grows a flower and the gardener cuts the flower so that the plant will strengthen its roots and grow many flowers. If the plant could feel (like an adolescent, for example), it would think that its first flower is the only flower that it will ever have. If the first flower is not cut, the plant will become impoverished and unable to reach its full potential. It is through castration, signifying what is the law and what is forbidden, that the subject comes to know and reinforce his desires. The law signified by the adult is not a repressive law *per se*, but is the law that is respected and upheld by the adult world and the "castrating" parent. If this is not the case, according to Dolto, then perversion might result, especially if the castrating adult is motivated not by the law common to all, but by his or her own narcissistic needs.

Symbolic castrations that form the individual are basically situated at the Freudian stages of development, beginning with birth, the umbilical castration, then oral, anal, and genital castrations. Each one is elaborated by Dolto from the child's perspective and from that of the adult. The "castrations" become symbolic when their function is to help the child give up old and outdated modes of realising his desires in order to embrace new, more mature strategies that allow him to progress towards ever greater accomplishments of his sexual potential. Her term *allant, devenant dans la genie de son sexe* is Dolto's very personal expression that each human being is in constant evolution towards the realisation of himself or herself as a sexual being. Her optimistic vision of human development places the "death instinct" within this positive dynamic as a necessary element of the life processes. Whereas Freud understood the "death instinct" within the contexts of war and destruction, Dolto insists that the death instinct has nothing to do with war and destruction—these belong to the life instincts and aggressiveness. On the contrary, for Dolto, the death instinct, when linked to the life instinct, is a necessary support of social life, a protection against the domination of individualistic narcissism.

Following Freud's theory of ambivalence due to the split between the life and death instincts, Dolto's work on primary narcissism is interesting to note. According to her, during this phase of development, before the "mirror stage" (Dolto, 1984, p. 147), when the child begins to gain a sense of his/her own body as separate from that of the mother, the death instinct of the parents can be very dangerous for the child, because it can prevent the formation of the body image. Should the parents not have desired the child, or a part of the child for whom they have negative feelings, the death instinct can impede the child's access to symbolisation and language.

> If the subject is denied his/her symbolic value, the death instinct will tend to override the life instinct . . . if desire is not imbedded within the life instinct, then the life instinct that prevails will not be in the direction of humanisation. (Dolto 2005, p. 38)

Dolto's work with psychotic children produced many of her original and rich clinical theories. For example, she claims that at the pregenital stage of development, in the case of early childhood psychosis, it is as if the ocean (to continue the metaphor of the life and death instincts) remained flat and undisturbed, with no differentiating waves formed. It is as if the child had not been able to value his/her body image as a human being and, therefore, did not become an autonomous individual. As children who, at the Oedipus stage, had not "valued their sex", they saw themselves as human beings, but remained undifferentiated sexually. Therefore, they could not experience primary castration or Oedipal development. Inspired by Freud's theories of sexual development, Dolto applied these in her own way to understanding childhood psychosis through her clinical work with very regressed children.

Just as Dolto's ocean represents her curiosity of where the dead go, so Sandor Ferenczi's *Thalassa: A Theory of Genitality* begins with the "riddle of how the child comes to be in the mother's body". Unlike his other writings, based on clinical work, *Thalassa* seems to be more of a philosophical *phantasia*, where he allows his imagination to run free. Why did he write *Thalassa*? Faced with my own difficulties with this text, I would ask for your indulgence in what I am about to reveal of my own free-floating thoughts and reading of *Thalassa*. First of all, to come back to Freud's "oceanic feelings", to Dolto's "wave and ocean", and to Ferenczi's "thalassa", are we not facing the process of "symbolic construction" in the desperate effort of finding a legitimate epistemological status for psychoanalysis? Is this not exactly what we are struggling with today—how to justify the status of psychoanalysis and protect it from the onslaught of cognitive, biochemical, medical, market-orientated, and symbolic arguments?

Ferenczi began thinking about *Thalassa* in 1915, during the First World War, when he was a young soldier translating Freud's text, *Three Essays on the Theory of Sexuality* (1905d). It was during this period that "psychoanalysis" was called upon officially to serve as a tool for understanding "war trauma". Army officials were present at the first congress in Budapest on war trauma. Psychoanalysis had now joined the public domain. This must have been an ultimate moment of satisfaction for Freud, but also the beginning of a life of never-ending stress. Stress still plagues psychoanalysts today, as we defend the "truth criterion" of this very human and, therefore, threatening field of study. What is more important than to know and understand the mystery of human life?

Ferenczi proposes to explore "the meaning and explanation of the phenomena of the act of coitus itself", beginning with the biological concept of the fusion of egg and sperm (*amphimixis*), which he then

extends to urethral and anal erotisms. He begins his text by epistemological reflections about using scientific explanations for mental
phenomena, or analogies as tools for understanding. He is encouraged by Freud's having been compelled to reduce mental functioning
to topographical, dynamic, economic, and, therefore, purely physical
processes, "for otherwise he was unable to approach their final explanation". He goes on to say, "I perceived that we need not be ashamed
of this reciprocal analogising, that on the contrary it should be vigorously pushed as a highly necessary and indeed, inevitable method"
(Ferenczi, 1989, p. 3). Is it this newly found bravery that allows him
the freedom to examine "coitus" and "thalassa" with new metaphors
and analogies?

Time does not allow me to explore *Thalassa* in further detail, and
how Ferenczi makes his way from the biological to the symbolic, but
I think that a quote from his "bioanalytical conclusions" summarises
his position:

> A not less significant, although at first blush certainly very surprising,
> methodological departure which we have permitted ourselves in this
> work has been the utilization of symbolism as a source of knowledge
> in the sphere of natural science. By conceiving of the 'symbols' which
> can be analytically recognized as such in the content of the psyche—
> by conceiving of these as not fortuitous and sportive expression
> of phantasy activity, but rather the historically significant traces of
> 'repressed' biological situations, we arrived at fundamentally new and
> perhaps not wholly erroneous assumptions regarding the meaning of
> genitality in general and of a number of its individual manifestations.
> One can scarcely predict the further developments of which this point
> of view may be capable, or how much unconscious wisdom lies
> concealed in the naive tradition of folklore, of *Märchen* and of myths,
> and in particular in the luxuriant symbolism of dreams. (Ferenczi,
> 1989, p. 87)

To conclude, we have seen how both Françoise Dolto and Sandor
Ferenczi fought for the legitimacy of psychoanalysis as a humanistic,
and humanising, symbolic order of thought and practice. Perhaps
more than Freud, they were not ready to compromise what they felt
to be an ethical position, which contributed to the "marginalisation"
of both within mainstream psychoanalysis. Dolto and Ferenczi practised and developed psychoanalysis as a craft in the noble sense of the

word: they learned the trade from their mentors within an ethical frame upon which each could build with her/his own intuition and creativity. Both separated from their mentors for ethical reasons; both felt that their mentors had deviated from their own symbolic values. Did Dolto's popularisation of psychoanalysis threaten the status of the analyst? Did Ferenczi's active methods and insistence on the role of countertransference make psychoanalysis less "scientifically" legitimate? How are we, the present generation of psychoanalysts, going to fight for the right of psychoanalysis to survive as a human, symbolic activity in a world of virtual reality and human mutation?

For my final words, I would like to quote the late Serge Leclaire, a friend and a respected Lacanian. In a speech he gave before a government commission on the status of psychoanalysis, he said,

It simply involves recognizing that the object of the human sciences in general and of psychoanalysis in particular has its own consistency, which depends on a non-ideological conceptual elaboration that is neither religious nor metaphysical or scientific; that is to say, an elaboration which is pertinent to the realities it addresses; realities which essentially consist of relationships; phantasies, drives and desires, among terms which can be conceptualised but not objectified: subject (of desire), (unconscious) thought, object (of the drive). Psychoanalysis is a systematic approach to a space made up of dimensions other than those that account for the geometry of a three or four dimensional world. The reality of this no less 'natural' space is made of 'dimensions' (memory, forgetting, drives, desires) for which the categories of quantity and measure are not pertinent. The concepts derive from phenomena such as repetitions, resistances, memory lapses, reminiscences, mutations, spotted '*in vivo*' in the unfolding of the cure, which allow the extraction of structural constants, of specific conditions of interactions, and more generally of the elaboration (keeping to my scientific metaphors) of a physiology of the signifier which more closely resembles a hyper complex and unstable immunological system than a pyramidal and unifying explanatory system. (Leclaire, 2000)

References

Dolto, F. (1984). *L'image inconsciente du corps*. Paris: Editions du Seuil.
Dolto, F. (1986). *Enfances*. Paris: Editions du Seuil.

Dolto, F. (1989). *Autoportrait d'une Psychanalyste 1934–1988* Edition du Seuil, Paris

Dolto, F. (2005). *La vague et l'océan: seminaire sur la pulsion de mort, 1970–71.* Paris: Editions Gallimard.

Ferenczi, S. (1929). The unwelcome child and the death instinct. In: *Final Contributions to the Problems and Methods of Psychoanalysis* (p. 102). London: Hogarth Press.

Ferenczi, S. (1932). *The Clinical Diary of Sándor Ferenczi,* J. Dupont (Ed.), M. Balint & N. Z. Jackson (Trans.). Cambridge, MA: Harvard University Press, 1995.

Ferenczi, S. (1955). Confusion of tongues between adults and the child. In: *Final Contributions to the Problems and Methods of Psycho-analysis* (p. 156). London: Hogarth Press.

Ferenczi, S. (1989). *Thalassa: A Theory of Genitality,* H. A. Bunker (Trans.). London: Maresfield Library, Karnac.

Freud, S. (1905d). *Three Essays on the Theory of Sexuality.* S.E., 7: 125–245. London: Hogarth.

Leclaire, S. (2000). *Etats des lieux de la psychanalyse.* Paris: Albin Michel.

PART III

THE BALINTS—MEMORIES, PERSONAL RECOLLECTIONS AND IMAGES FROM LONDON, PARIS, AND BUDAPEST[1]

Note

1. Editors' note: Several chapters in this section are personal reminiscences rather than conventional papers; for these, bibliographies are included instead of formal references.

CHAPTER FIVE

Michael Balint

Harold Stewart

W e are devoting this section to the work of Michael Balint and two of his wives, Alice and Enid. Judith Dupont will discuss Alice, Hidas will talk about Mészáros Street 12, Jennifer Johns will review Enid and Catherine Reverzy, and I, Michael.

I first met him in the 1950s at the Tavistock Clinic, when I went to see him for advice on psychotherapy training. He was then a solid middle-aged man with a marked Hungarian accent and a direct and forthright manner. When he later supervised my psychoanalytical training case, I came to value this directness, together with his ability to admit error: yet others occasionally found him rather bullying, particularly in seminars. However, we all accepted his capacity to challenge and question everything, never to take things for granted in order to help people to think for themselves. You either loved him or hated him. You could not be indifferent.

He was born in 1896 in Budapest into a medical family, his father being a general practitioner. He qualified in medicine, developed a liking for psychoanalysis, and went into analysis with Hanns Sachs in Berlin. Feeling dissatisfied with Sachs, he returned to Budapest for analysis with Ferenczi, a man Balint revered all his life. He came to England in 1939 and he, together with Klein, Winnicott, Bion, and

Fairbairn, became one of the progenitors of the British Object Relations School. He became a President of the British Society, but died of a heart attack in 1970 while in office.

His theories and concepts developed over a period of some forty years, culminating in a degree of integration in his last book, *The Basic Fault* (1979). Some of his most important contributions to theory and technique lie within the concept of regression, particularly in its use as a therapeutic agent, containing the pioneering and controversial work of Ferenczi in this area. Regression to more primitive methods of mental functioning is intimately associated with theories of the development of object relations in infancy. He introduced the concept of the new beginning, of learning new ways of relating and discarding compulsive pathological patterns, a concept similar to working through, mourning, and reparation. He described his clinical experience of working with regressed patients and the problems he encountered leading up to his major contribution in the field, the distinction between two types of regression, between benign and malignant regression, of regression in the interests of recognition and regression in the interest of gratification.

He looked at regression from its theoretical aspect concerning its relationship to the influence of the early forms of object-relations upon the individual psyche. He strongly disagreed with Freud's concept of primary narcissism and was the first to argue that narcissism is always a secondary phenomenon. For him, as with Ferenczi, the relationship to the mother is primary, a basic biological and psychological given, and, following Ferenczi, described it as passive object-love, the need to be loved unconditionally by the mother. Subsequently, together with Alice Balint, he recognised that the infant, far from being passive, was healthily active, and so changed the concept from passive to primary object-love. At a later stage, he described this state as a harmonious mix-up of subject and object, a feeling of unity with the object, and suggested that incitable frustrations and separations will destroy this unity, resulting in the emergence of discrete firm objects. In *Thrills and Regressions* (1959), he postulated that in response to these traumatic events the infant might develop in the direction of what he termed *ocnophilia* and *philobatism* in its object-relations. In ocnophilia, objects are experienced as safe and friendly, whereas the space between objects is threatening and hostile; in philobatism, the reverse is the case.

Michael Balint with his grandchildren and the Dupont children.

His theorising has so far been concerned with vicissitudes of loving and of the libido, but he now suggests a theory of hate. In his opinion, and contrary to Freud's, hate is always of a secondary reactive nature and is not one of the constituents of the basic primary drives. Fairbairn is the only other theorist of this School who has a similar view.

In a later development, Balint adds another stage between primary love and ocnophilia–philobatism, and this is the stage of the basic fault. He regards it as a structural deficiency, arising from intense discrepancies between the infant's biopsychological needs and the maternal care of the primary objects. It is to these early traumatic experiences and the associated phantasies that regressions occurred in future psychopathologies. This concept of deficiency has been used particularly by Winnicott, and also by Bion, in their theorising on maternal deficiencies in two-person relationships.

In later years, Balint put forward a new theory of the three areas of the mind based on one-, two-, and three-person relationships. The one-person relationship is described as the area of creation, which concerns artistic and scientific creativity, among other phenomena; the two-person is the area of the basic fault where the dynamic force is not conflict but deficiency; and the three-person has the area of Oedipal conflict as its dynamic force.

His final contribution to psychoanalytic theory is a new theory of trauma, based once again on Ferenczi's views: those of traumatogenesis in childhood. There are the same three phases, the child–adult trust, the overstimulation of the child by the adult, followed by the adult's indifference to the child, which result in the traumatic experience.

Psychoanalytic technique was of special interest to him. He was one of the earliest analysts to discuss countertransferences, again following in Ferenczi's footsteps. He came to regard it as the totality of the analyst's behaviour and professional attitude towards the patient. The analyst's task is to help create and maintain the analytical situation by means of the analytic language used, his set of terms and concepts used in constructing interpretations. It includes the emotional tensions aroused, the necessary frustrations and satisfactions needed to maintain an optimal level, and the creating of an atmosphere to enable patients to express themselves optimally. Balint strongly believed that regression in analysis is not merely a defence against the here-and-now of the analytic relationship, but is a most important communication of a state of mind concerned with deeply repressed traumatic experiences and the unconscious phantasies and defences associated with them. He put forward the concepts of the unobtrusive analyst for the creation of this appropriate atmosphere and of the analyst's indestructibility, the latter concept also associated with Winnicott and Bion.

Balint, however, recognised, as Ferenczi apparently had not, that some regressed patients do not enter into a benign constructive state but, instead, enter into malignant destructive addiction-like states, where the sole interest of the patient is on instinctual gratification of his id wishes, rather than insight. The analyst's task is to try to understand and to prevent this from occurring, if possible, with the technical tools available to him, limited as they might be.

We now turn to the field of applied psychoanalysis, where Balint's major contribution was to the field of general medical practice. Here, he was following not only in Ferenczi's footsteps, but also his father's. First in Budapest and later in London, he established discussion groups for doctors who were interested in the emotional problems of their patients, with the group's aim being one of research-cum-training. His major account of this work was in his book, *The Doctor, His Patient and The Illness* (1957), which made him internationally famous among doctors. His basic premise was that any emotion felt by the doctor in his immediate relationship with the patient needed to be regarded as a symptom of the patient's illness—a very original use of countertransference. These groups are now known as "Balint groups" and, in 1969, the Balint Society was instituted to continue his work under the leadership of his wife, Enid. In addition to doctors, this discussion group format was used by Michael and Enid with psychiatric colleagues in the National Health Service to study brief focal psychotherapy techniques, with doctors and nurses in the Family Planning Association, now the Institute of Psychosexual Medicine, and with social workers in marital work, now the Institute of Marital Studies. This is a formidable contribution to the mental health of Great Britain.

In conclusion, we note that although Balint's work has been somewhat neglected since his death, more recently it seems to have been coming to the fore again, with the publication in the USA, under the guest editorship of Judith Dupont, of three issues of the *American Journal of Psychoanalysis*, devoted to Balint's life and work. Like Ferenczi, his contribution is again becoming established and valued in the psychoanalytic world.

Bibliography

Balint, A. (1952). Love for the mother and mother love. In: M. Balint (Ed.), *Primary Love and Psychoanalytic Technique* (pp. 251–259). London: Hogarth Press.

Balint, M. (1957). *The Doctor, His Patient and the Illness*. London: Pitman Medical Publishing.

Balint, M. (1959). *Thrills and Regressions*. London: Hogarth Press.

Balint, M. (1979). *The Basic Fault*, New York: Brunner/Mazel.

The American Journal of Psychoanalysis, 62(1 & 4), 2002, and 63(3), 2003.

CHAPTER SIX

The Balints and Mészáros Street 12, Budapest

György Hidas

I t is a great honour for me to have the opportunity to recall the Budapest years of Michael Balint. I begin with some personal and subjective memories. As a junior high school student, age ten, I was a classmate of John Balint, Michael's son, in a school in an inner district of Buda, until the Balints emigrated to England in 1939. During the winter, John and I skated together in the City Park, and I saw Michael Balint several times when he came by car to fetch his son from the skating rink. "What a lucky boy," I thought, "his father drives him home."

I played often with John and other children in the Balint home. I was impressed not only by his miniature train and ship models, but by the intellectual and artistic environment as well. When I learned that the parents were psychoanalysts, all my visual impressions were interspersed with this somewhat mysterious profession. As I realised later, when I studied psychoanalysis, their house at Mészáros Street 12 was famous. The house was owned by the Kovács family. Vilma Kovács, also an analysand of Ferenczi, was the mother of Alice Balint. It was in this building that the Psychoanalytic Institute and Clinic, directed first by Ferenczi and later by Balint, was subsequently housed. Perhaps these impressions contributed to my early decision to become a psychoanalyst.

Sisters Olga Székely-Kovács and Alice Balint outside Mészáros Street 12
in Budapest.

Let me cite two memories concerning Michael Balint and his
father. I quote Imre Hermann, the famous Hungarian psychoanalyst:

> the father of Michael Balint, Dr Bergsmann, was a practitioner in
> District Eight in Budapest. I was his patient. When I was nine years
> old, he treated my broken arm. He was an angry man, but he must
> have treated me well because I have good memories of him and I was
> not afraid of him.

Another memory by Hermann:

> In August 1919, I met Misi Balint in an apartment of a professor at the
> university, where both of us sought refuge. Misi worked in a chemi-
> cal laboratory. He was younger than me by seven years. I was an assis-
> tant at the psychological institute. Both of us were targets of the attack
> of racist, right-wing university students. We could get away though
> and saw in our escape a kind of good beginning. Our common fate
> had brought us together; we became good friends forever.

Hermann was the older, yet it was he who had to write his memories of Balint after his friend's death in 1970.

Michael Balint graduated from the Budapest Medical School in 1918. There he attended Ferenczi's psychoanalytical lectures in the short period in 1919 when Ferenczi was professor of psychoanalysis. This was the first encounter of the two men. At this time, Balint's interest was focused on Freud's *Three Essays on Sexuality* and on *Totem and Taboo*. After the counter-revolution, he and his wife, Alice Balint, moved to Berlin. His first analyst was Hanns Sachs, but Balint found him too didactic. The Balints returned to Budapest and, in the period between 1924 and 1926, he was analysed by Ferenczi. At this time, Balint worked in a biochemical laboratory. In the subsequent years, he was a research assistant at the Internal Medicine Department of the Budapest Medical School. In 1926, when a theory of genitality, *Thalassa*, was published in a Hungarian translation, Ferenczi asked Balint to review the manuscript from the viewpoint of modern biological thinking.

During his Budapest years, Balint had several publications in Hungarian medical journals, such as "Perversion or hysterical symptom" (1925), "Psychoanalysis and internal medicine, about psychotherapy for the practising doctor" (1926), and "Crisis of the medical practice" (1930). These papers were the precursors of his later seminal works, like *The Doctor, His Patient and The Illness*. In 1932, he wrote for *Imago* on "Psychosexual parallels to the bioenergetic fundamental law". The year of 1933 witnessed his paper "On transference" in the Hungarian medical journal *Gyógyászat*, and a more fundamental one, "Character analysis and new beginning", in the Ferenczi memorial volume. "New beginning" can happen in a trustful, fearless, unsuspicious object relation. In 1933, he also published a paper, "Ferenczi as medical doctor". Between 1935 and 1939, Balint wrote his important paper "Early developmental steps of the ego: primary object love", published in the *International Journal of Psychoanalysis*, and, together with Alice Balint, he wrote "On transference and counter-transference" for the same journal.

After his years at the Internal Medicine Department, he began his private psychoanalytic practice at Mészáros Street 12. This was the house where the Psychoanalytical Institute and Clinic was founded in 1931. Balint was first the deputy director of the Clinic, then the director, until his emigration from Hungary in 1939.

Inner courtyard of the building at Mészáros Street 12 (photo by András Kovács).

Now my private practice is in a neighbourhood close by. On my way there, I regularly pass this historic building.

Bibliography

Balint, A., & Balint M. (1939). On transference and counter-transference. *International Journal of Psychoanalysis, 20*: 233.

Balint, M. (1949). Early development states of the ego: primary object love. *International Journal of Psychoanalysis, 30*: 265.

Balint, M. (1957). *The Doctor, His Patient and The Illness*. London: Pitman Medical.

Balint M. (1965). Character analysis and new beginning. In: *Primary Love and Psychoanalytical Technique*. London: Tavistock.

Ferenczi, S. (1934). *Lélekelemzési tanulmányok* (Memorial Volume). Budapest: Somlo Bela.

Ferenczi, S. (1989). *Thalassa: A Theory of Genitality*. London: Karnac.

CHAPTER SEVEN

Alice Balint, a short but productive life

Judith Dupont

I f one walks around Buda, and climbs to the top of the Naphegy, Mount Sun, there is a nice round park. At the corner of this park and the street called Orvos utca, the Doctor street, there is a huge building of glass and metal, not at all in harmony with the rest of the houses. Before 1945, instead of this building, there was a nice house surrounded by a garden. It was the home of the architect, Frederic Kovács, who lived there with his wife Vilma and the three children Vilma had with her first husband, Lajos Székely.

Vilma had been married, against her will, at the age of fifteen, to a man more than twenty years older then she. She had three children in three years, Alice, Olga, and Ferenc. Exhausted by her three pregnancies, she became very ill with tuberculosis, and had to enter a sanatorium, leaving her children with her elder sister. There she met a man of her own age, Frederic Kovács, and they fell in love. She wanted a divorce, but her husband refused. Nevertheless, she left him, and thus was blamed for the separation. The children remained with their father, and Vilma had no right to see them. She refused to accept this and met them almost every day on their way home from school, to see and talk with them.

On the terrace of the Kovács villa on Naphegy, Budapest. From left to right, Olga, Alice, composer Leo Weiner, Vilma, Frigyes, and music teacher Margit Varro.

The children were unhappy with their father, who was almost never at home. When Alice was eleven, she decided to run away with her sister and brother to live with their mother. Their father never made any attempt to get them back or even to see them again.

After the traumatic events she experienced, Vilma became ill with agoraphobia. Near the end of the First World War, she went into psychoanalytic treatment with Sandor Ferenczi.

During her treatment, which apparently was quite successful, Ferenczi became aware of the intelligence and sensibility of his patient. He encouraged her to pursue psychoanalytic training. So Vilma became a psychoanalyst, and a collaborator of Ferenczi. Together they invented the Hungarian system of analytic training and Vilma organised the clinical seminars in her house on the Naphegy.

The Kovács house was a kind of a cultural centre. On Sundays, one could meet there the painter Robert Berény, the music composer Leo Weiner, Grete Varró (director of a well known music school) and some of her pupils, like Louis Kentner, as well as Sandor and Gizella Ferenczi and their family.

It was a very stimulating environment for the children. Their stepfather adopted them as soon as it became possible, and took charge of their studies. Alice was a brilliant pupil. She was a schoolmate of

Emmi Bergsmann, sister of Michael Bergsmann, later known as Michael Balint. A third brilliant student also attended the same class—Margit Schönberger, later known as Margaret Mahler.

At university, Alice studied mathematics and anthropology. She was very interested in her mother's profession, and read all the psychoanalytic literature Vilma possessed. She lent Michael, a medical student with manifold interests, the *Three Essays* and *Totem and Taboo*, and he, too, became interested in psychoanalysis.

They soon decided to marry, and went to Berlin for psychoanalytic training. They started analysis with Hanns Sachs, but were dissatisfied with his overly intellectual approach; they returned to Budapest in order to pursue their analysis with Ferenczi. Some months later, Alice gave birth to their son, John.

Alice and Michael became active members of the Hungarian Psychoanalytic Society, and worked there until the beginning of 1939. Most of their work was the result of shared thoughts and discussion. As Michael wrote in the introduction to *Primary Love and Psychoanalytic Technique*,

> Starting with our shared enthusiasm for *Totem and Taboo* till her death in 1939, Alice and I read, studied, lived and worked together. All our ideas – no matter in whose mind they had first arisen – were enjoyed and then tested, probed and criticized in our endless discussions.

Alice Balint at the piano with Olga Székely-Kovács at home in 1927.

Quite often it was just chance that decided which of us should publish a particular idea. Apart from psychoanalysis, Alice's main interests were anthropology and education, mine biology and medicine, and usually this factor decided who should write about the idea. We published only one paper jointly, although almost all of them could have been printed under our joint names.

After the invasion of Austria by the Germans, they began investigating the possibility of leaving Hungary where the position of Jews—even if converted Christians—was becoming more and more difficult. In January 1939, the Balints left Hungary for England, and settled in Manchester. They had just begun to feel at home there when Alice, who was suffering from an aortic aneurysm ignored by everyone but Michael and herself, died suddenly in the first days of August, two days before the beginning of the Second World War. Her mother, Vilma Kovács, only survived her by nine months: she died in May of the following year.

Alice started to write and to publish during her stay in Berlin. Her first two papers, both published in the journal *Imago*, were still anthropologic papers. The first, in 1923, examines the place of man and woman in Mexican culture: through these war representations, she tries to draw some conclusions about them concerning human psychology in general. This study is still somewhat scholastic, but one can perceive in it something of her developing originality.

The second of these papers, "The pater familias", is based on her studies of North American Indian cultures. Here, psychoanalytic thinking is clearly prevalent over the anthropologic point of view.

As Balint writes in his introduction to *Primary Love and Psychoanalytic Technique*, Alice's main interest, besides anthropology, was the field of childhood education. Her first purely psychoanalytical work is a book, written in 1931, titled *Psychology of the Nursery*, with an introduction by Sandor Ferenczi. She describes, with many clinical examples, the development of the child—the problems encountered in various stages and their psychological meaning—and she gives the psychoanalyst's point of view of all these events. The book was quite a success, and was immediately translated into German and French. Her vision, as well as her style, is remarkably modern for a book written some seventy years ago. It is for that reason the book was republished in the 1950s in English, in the 1960s in German, in the 1990s in French, and recently in Hungarian.

She approaches the subject under the following headings: "Nursery and grown-ups", "The education of instincts", "The Oedipus complex", "The castration complex", "Identification: the conquest of the external world", "The child and his educators", and, in conclusion, "The child's liberation". In an appendix, she includes "The fundamentals of our education". As Alice Balint shows us, the nursery is the place where a primitive being is transformed into a civilised human, not without some considerable strain for the child as well as for the adults around him. Psychoanalysis can be of much help in understanding the special language of the nursery and in resolving some of the strains. The book deals with a problem that occupied Michael Balint until his last book, *The Basic Fault*: the interrelationship between the child's needs and the more or less well-adjusted responses of those who care for him. Today, it is recognised that the inadequacy of the responses to the child's needs is responsible for the most common traumas which unavoidably occur during the development of every human being and determines his "basic fault".

Of course, Alice Balint's book is the writing of a middle-class woman of the 1930s, written for other middle-class women, the only ones in a position to read it. But the author's analyses go deep enough to retain their complete value for present-day readers of any milieu. Today, some simplified psychoanalytic concepts are familiar to most people, but all child psychologists could attest to the extraordinary general misunderstanding of these concepts on the part of people who think they know them so well. Alice Balint's explanations are simple but never simplifying, deep, but always very clear.

Besides *Psychology of the Nursery*, Alice Balint's pedagogical work consists mostly of short papers written for educational journals or conferences for parents. Two titles, "Forbidding and allowing" and "The bases of our educational system" (1937), were presented to psychoanalytical conferences, in Wiesbaden, and to the second conference of the Four Nations. Other works include "Thumb sucking", "Excessive masturbation", and "What kind of tales to tell and when" (or "How and when to inform the child").

Alice Balint also published or presented some papers on psychoanalytic theory. The first of them, "Development of the feeling of love and sense of reality", appeared in a volume of the collected writings of Hungarian analysts, planned for a book to be published for Sandor Ferenczi's sixtieth birthday. Though Ferenczi died some weeks before his sixtieth birthday, the book was published, under the title *Psycho-analytical Studies*.

Alice presented her second psychoanalytic paper, "The management of transference on the bases of the Ferenczian experiences", at the first conference of the Four Nations. In this paper, she deals with the problems of transference and countertransference, considered from a Ferenczian point of view, but in her own original manner.

Her last two theoretical papers were presented at a seminar in Manchester: these were "The superego" and "Repression". She approaches these two classical notions in her very lively and precise way, giving enlightening examples. One can perceive in them the anthropological as well as the pedagogical sensibility.

Just like Michael Balint, Alice was also very interested in the psychological aspects of the mother–child relationship. The three papers she wrote on this subject are part of their common work. In 1933, she wrote "A specific form of the infantile fear", where she studies the fear of falling, of being dropped: that is, of losing the love of the mother. She makes the connection between her ideas and the theory of clinging according to Imre Hermann. One can discern in this paper the first steps in the thought process that later led Michael Balint to his idea of ocnophilic and philobatic regression. A second paper, "Considerations about parental love", was published in 1937, and the best known one, "Love of the mother and mother love", in 1939. This latter paper, written together with Michael, is part of the thought process that led him, some years later, to his last book, *The Basic Fault*, which sums up the essence of his life's work.

Alice Balint's psychoanalytic activity extended from her beginnings in Berlin in 1924 until her death in 1939, only fifteen years. In this relatively short time, she produced an abundant and rich body of work, which is still insufficiently known and recognised.

Bibliography

Balint, A. (1921). Die mexichanische Kriegsshieroglyphe (Mexican War Hieroglyph). *Imago*, 9: 401–407.

Balint, A. (1926). Der Familienvater (Pater familias). *Imago*, 12: 292–304.

Balint, A. (1935). Mikor és mit mesélünk? (When and what do we tell?). In: *Gyermeknevelés*, 1: 14–17.

Balint, A. (1941). Az elfojtásrol (On repression). In: *Anya és Gyermek, Tanulmányok* (pp. 7–35). Budapest: Pantheon.

Balint, A. (1941). A Felettes énről (On superego). In: *Anya és Gyermek, Tanulmányok* (pp. 21–36). Budapest: Pantheon.

Balint, A. (1941). A fokozottan onanizáló gyermek (On excessive masturbation). In: *Gyermeknevelés II, Anya és Gyermek, Tanulmányok.* Budapest: Pantheon.

Balint, A. (1955). *The Psychoanalysis of the Nursery.* London: Tavistock Publications.

Balint, A. (1971). Due Grundlagen unseres Erziehungsssytems (Fundamentals of our education system). In: J. Cremerius, *Psychoanalyse und Erziehungspraxis* (Psychoanalysis and Education). Frankfurt: Fischer..

Balint, A. (1971). Versagen und Gewahren in der Erziehung (Failure and perception in education). In: J. Cremerius, *Psychoanalyse und Erziehungspraxis* (Psychoanalysis and Education). Frankfurt: Fischer.

Balint, M. (1952). *Primary Love and Psychoanalytic Technique.* London: Hogarth Press.

Balint, M. (1979). *The Basic Fault.* New York: Brunner/Mazel.

Cremerius, J. (1971). *Psychoanalyse und Erziehungspraxis* (Psychoanalysis and Education). Frankfurt: Fischer.

Ferenczi Memorial Volume (1934). *Lélekelemzési tanulmányok* (Psychoanalytical Studies). Budapest: Somló Béla.

CHAPTER EIGHT

Thrills and progression: Hillary, a philobat on Mount Everest[1]

Catherine Reverzy

B alint and Ferenczi inspired me to write my book *Femmes d'aventure* (Reverzy, 2001) about risk-taking, motivation, and self-real-
isation. Intended for a broader public, it draws on my personal
encounters with, and readings of, renowned female navigators,
climbers, pilots, and explorers. In this chapter, I examine both the
attraction to, and the fear of, adventure and the unknown. I am also
looking at one's capacity for facing danger and returning unharmed
to share the experience.

What is the spirit of adventurousness? To understand such a state
of mind, it seems necessary to go far back into early childhood, where
our primitive yet determining attitudes towards the world are shaped.
I have chosen a psychoanalytic viewpoint—though other perspectives
could be equally valid. Within this context, I have looked to Balint,
whose original and fascinating work presented in *Thrills and
Regression* (1959), was a great help in my explorations. Balint mentions
outdoor sports, and climbing in particular. Several times he quotes
Hillary, who conquered Mount Everest in 1953, only a few years prior
to the publication of Balint's book.

Hillary describes his Sherpa,[2] Tensing Norgay, as a "paternal
figure worthy of trust" and as the good philobat, Hillary leaned on
this paternal figure's guidance in reaching the summit.

What can we learn from them?

In *Thrills and Regression*, Balint establishes links between ways of relating to the world and the earliest primitive life experiences. He tries to outline the conditions for a newborn baby's well-being, distress, and all those sensorial experiences which can either create (engender) or dissipate primitive anxiety. Like Ferenczi, he explicitly refers to the "clinging instinct", a term coined by Imre Hermann and developed further by authors such as Spitz and Bowlby. The concept refers to attachment, and has given rise to a number of works on early infantile relationship between mother and child, including birth and intrauterine life. The ethological works of Boris Cyrulnik (2005), for instance, focused on diverse forms of primitive links: security, anxiety, escapism, ambivalence, and resilience.

Balint shows a specific interest in funfairs. Among the pleasures to be experienced there, he explores those causing a sensation of vertigo: swings, wild rides, and roller-coasters. One year earlier, French sociologist Roger Caillois published his *Des Jeux et des Hommes*, in which he studied vertigo games calling them "ilynx", a name derived from the Greek "whirlpool" (in English, Caillois, 1961).

According to Balint, these new forms of activity provide increasingly complex and diverse stimulation, leading to the experience of vertigo and other extreme sensory sensations. Sailing, piloting, jumping, diving, training wild animals, exploratory journeys to unknown territories and untouched lands, all deserve attention. He considers these repetitive activities to be tolerable abreactions of the original trauma and believes that they foster the capacity of mastering traumatic situations. This capacity is unconsciously strengthened by a partial restoration of the sensation of the "harmonious mix" we are familiar with from our intrauterine life.

Observing adult behaviour towards risk-taking and extreme sport activities, Balint contemplates both the pleasure of the individual constantly seeking "new thrills" and the fear of those who cannot even contemplate such foolhardiness.

Fifty years later, Balint's observations are evermore up to date. Funfairs multiply; rides continue to be more and more sophisticated. Accidents related to roller-coasters, which now reach accelerations of 3 or 4g, are on the rise. Four million French people aged twenty to thirty qualify as "adrenalin junkies", and the same goes for other western nations. More and more people, as Balint foresaw, expose themselves deliberately to situations bringing about the experience of anxiety related to the loss of balance, stability, and contact with the ground. Alpinism and extreme winter sports, as well as trekking in the desert, jungle, or at the poles, are all becoming popular activities. Amid Spartan conditions, thousands of youthful city-dwellers find pleasure in the outdoors and in defying the elements. By escaping routine and the boredom of overwhelming security, they rejuvenate themselves and reclaim the joy of life.

However, the majority of us will never leave our comfort zone or the confines of our protected lives, and carefully avoid anything that could upset our routine.

With Balint's exploration of the "psychology of thrills", especially pleasures associated with vertigo, fascinating parallels can be drawn with Roger Caillois' contributions, making us aware that certain play activities aimed at stimulating the inner ear can be observed not only in different cultures, but also among animals.

Those who seek "intense thrills" go through three stages:

- fear—linked to being aware of danger
- pleasure—in deliberate risk taking
- confidence—in one's ability to return to a safety zone.

This sequence reminds us of the games of children. You leave the safety zone, take off to "friendly spaces" (in Ferenczi's words), and come back to base: this is hide and seek, cowboys and Indians, or imaginary travels through hostile territory. The scenario conjures up joy and excitement that defies fear. Rides and swings provide us with similar sensations. They are associated with the pleasure of vertigo and the near certitude of being caught by someone before falling. Such games—Balint maintains—revisit the sensorial experience of birth. Separation, situations of insecurity, and danger bring us back to this experience.

But why do some people expose themselves unnecessarily to real danger, while others would not contemplate such action? Why do some seek "shivers down their spines", while others get "cold feet"?

Balint created two words to describe such phenomena, ultimately related to our first relationship:

- ocnophile—describes someone "who likes to cling " (from the Greek *Okneo* to hold on to, but also to retract, to dread, to hesitate)

Sir Edmund Hillary.

- philobat—someone who enjoys walking on the edge, and goes for the limit, for example, an acrobat.

In the archaic period of the earliest days, a baby goes through cycles of clinging, separation, and reunion with the mother's body over and over again. These experiences are built into the psycho-biological (somato-psychic) base that will influence our later attitudes towards the unknown.

Balint's ocnophile and philobat use two different ways of approaching the state of "being loved in the world".

The ocnophile baby reacted to its first object, the mother, with an anxious and excessive grip. Why? The mother—powerless, stressed, or depressed—could not provide her baby with the basic security needed at the time. This child will know insecurity, incomprehension, and the lack of empathy. Growing up in fear and insecurity, the child will not be able to develop autonomy and independence and will consequently ensure that his or her objects stay close. Such children doubt all things, including themselves. Clumsy and stressed, they can only be reassured by the manifestations and contact of their objects. Eternally anticipating destabilising effects, in adulthood such people will appreciate boundaries, solid walls, accumulating consumer goods, as well as positions, titles, and ideologies, Balint says. Their world is sedentary, riddled by conventions and things that make them feel comfortable and safe. Balint asserts that the ocnophile ensures the smooth running of society, being prepared for any compromise in order to feel loved. The ocnophile's true goal is not only to cling, but also to be held without even having to express the desire for it.

This is exactly what the philobat had known as a baby.

Philobats had been held by their mother, as they needed to be. Their first months were peaceful and comfortable: they had a "good enough" mother. Given that they had been able to develop autonomy, they are able to move on and leave their objects with ease. They go forth, enjoy exploring the unknown, take pleasure in novel experiences as well as in solitude, and enjoy returning *home*. They love destabilising themselves and losing landmarks while playing: they are sure to find them again. The philobat nurtures adventurous dreams and anticipates departure.

We will see how much Hillary remembers having been like that as a child.

Philobats experience fear, but they are geared towards action: fear pushes them forward towards "friendly spaces". Even though the road might be littered with dangerous objects, they will conquer them. "Everything will be all right", they say to themselves, "I am sure of making it safely". Uncertain horizons are open to them: skies, oceans, eternal snows, and the great outdoors. All that is blurry and unpredictable enables them to mobilise their intelligence and adaptation skills. This is the philobat's "element". Balint gives us several examples: "the security of the pilot in the skies, the sailor on high seas, the skier on the slopes . . ." He underlines that if the ocnophile's world is that of touch and physical proximity to the object of safety, in the philobat's world a good distance and a compulsive need to survey the environment is essential.

Even though they love to distance themselves from their anchor, philobats are not without bonds. They are by no means asocial. Amenable to others, extroverted, they can be good team players and know how to adapt. Hillary, the expedition leader, was such an example. Philobats do not like either solitude, or being excessively loved. Consequently, they do not always answer others' need for love and might appear selfish. However, they are grateful for the support of their family and friends, and know that they will be expecting their return. They count on their "good gear" to ensure both performance and survival: ropes, clasps, in fact any technology which will enable them to attain their goal and return from harm's way—rescued, if necessary.

For ocnophiles, all risk-taking can only end badly. They do not trust their guiding stars, their "baraka". In fact, they are quite right not to venture out. They would soon be in danger; their clumsiness and tendency to flee into introspection would impede the gesture that could save them.

Philobats, on the other hand, are self-confident and entrust the world they survey. Risk taking is calculated. Competent and astute, they evaluate situations rapidly, face them, fight and win: nevertheless, they also know how to retreat and flee if all else fails. They are not suicidal. They believe in their lucky stars, their "baraka".

With everyone and with the world, they maintain a bond of efficiency based on trust and vigilance: intelligent, well-trained and fit, all senses on the lookout, they achieve what they undertake. As for the obstacles they face on the road—storms, winds, animals, rocks, hostile populations—they master and control them, enjoying the pleasure of experiencing their strength and perfecting their skills.

On the mountain, the ocnophile finds the altitude and the storms overwhelming. The philobat admires the scenery. The ocnophile is constantly frightened of suffocation, falling, and annihilation.

This special ability is the essence of philobatism, writes Balint. The philobat knows—as the example of Hillary demonstrates—that any wrong move could prove disastrous. In moments of emergency, he is capable of finding an ocnophile object which he will cling to, and which will eventually save him. In situations of danger, he must be able to call upon his ocnophilia. Alpinists and climbers are fully aware of this truth.

We might add that this is precisely what the acrobat practises day by day.

Balint introduced the concepts of ocnophile and philobat more than fifty years ago. Here, they are used to open up a space for studying courage, audacity, fear, and our ability to master it. According to Balint, no one is entirely ocnophile or entirely philobat. In fact, these are attitudes, grown out of the same root, used by the psyche in variable proportions to deal with difficulties in our world of objects. We control their elasticity. Ocnophilia and philobatism both play a part in our survival and well-being. Ocnophilic fear enhancing the perception of danger compels careful behaviour and triggers an instinctive search for support and protection. It is complementary to philobatic aggression, which forces one to counter-attack and conquer, feeding the desire to win. The pleasure and joy of mastering one's fear is essentially philobatic in nature.

Enid Balint was interested in the relationship of time and space for both ocnophiles and philobats. In her opinion, the ocnophile dislikes and avoids distance between objects and satisfactions. The philobat, on the other hand, has managed to overcome his anxiety provoked by the time gap between satisfactions at an early age (Balint, 1959).

For Balint, these attitudes are not limited to the external physical world, but also apply to our relations to ideas and ideals.

Through my observations, I was also able to see the connection between philobatic components of one's personality and the essence of adventurousness—or "enterprising ability". The philobat approaches his goals with a deep commitment, involving his whole personality. Refusing to give up one's dreams without being lost in them, to be self-confident, to enjoy playing, to face extreme situations and to know how to return home, these are the characteristics that help the philobat realise his risky enterprises in their world, where the wind of freedom seems to blow.

In *Femmes d'aventure* (Reverzy, 2001), I emphasised that, for young people and practitioners of extreme sports, adventure is about a quest for oneself, for truth, and not simply for breaking records or becoming famous. I wished to show that the success of a risky expedition is always the end product of a long and patient personal journey, which is embedded in the complexity of the entire life story and has roots going back to childhood.

The first relationship might have been solid or fragile, either fostering or hindering the early development of basic security. It provides psycho-biological grounds for cohesion and the capacity of maintaining balance amid destabilising conditions. Balint emphasises that the "safety zone" bears permanent archaic traces of the primary object relationships that are decisive in the development of our sense of basic security (or insecurity). They are also responsible for one's ability to explore unknown, friendly or hostile spaces as well as one's need to cling to familiar and existing relationships.

Novel birthing techniques aim at creating such a sense of basic security. These techniques include giving birth in water, diminishing stress at birth and fostering positive bonding between the child and the mother. Of interest is the work on early prevention of insecure attachment modalities by Belgian obstetrician Dr Pierre Rousseau, known in France for his works on perinatal mourning. He emphasises the importance of the earliest visual interaction between the newborn and his mother taking place before the newborn finds the breast (Rousseau, 1995).

Though the philobat evokes the image of a person being strong and stable, Balint warns us that things are more complex: philobat patients suffer from an inability to build solid love relationships. He compares them to unflinching heroes like those of Jules Verne, or the knights who appear in children's dreams. He describes their heroism as "close to phallic–narcissistic auto-eroticism, puerile and virile", never entirely mature (Balint, M., 1959). He does not hide his reservations towards the human value of such achievements: "It is hard to explain to a sceptic what is the personal value attached to having climbed the highest summits or descend to the deepest abyss or the ocean floor" (Balint, M., 1959). In *Femmes d'aventure*, I became interested in investigating what such experiences mean for those who undertake them, and what we can learn from the specifically human desire to progress and incessantly redefine the boundaries of what is possible.

Ferenczi, preceding Balint, directed his attention to the universal appeal of dangerous, vertiginous, and thrilling games. In *Thalassa*, he writes that the sexual act

> reminds us of those melodramas in which, while there are of course dark clouds threatening all kinds of destruction just as in a real tragedy, there is always the feeling that 'everything will turn out all right'. (Ferenczi, 1989, p. 42)

In this everyday drama we can already recognise the complementarity of ocnophile and philobat. These attitudes appear secondary to a previous stage (which presents the common root referred to by Balint), the narcissistic sense of completeness experienced in the uterine world. Indeed, it is our arrival into the world which breaks that feeling, forcing us to live forever between clinging and separation. Perhaps we perpetually pursue a return to this lost wholeness. It seems to me that this search for the lost object resembles the "quest for the holy grail" which adventurers often talk about.

Both the horrifying empty spaces that drive the ocnophile to cling on, and the "friendly spaces" in which the philobat navigates and climbs, take us away from this intrauterine state. The never-ending quest is that of returning to prenatal harmony. A return to the "harmonious mix" depends on the philobat's ability to recreate in reality a little harmony of the friendly spaces that supported and enveloped him before discovering the world of separate objects. It is to the world of thalassa that the philobat regresses in his phantasy. Hence, the end sought by the philobat would seem to be "progressing into regression".

Ferenczi wrote in 1924,

> it is possible that the temporary return to the maternal womb and the simultaneous playful repetition and overcoming of all the dangers inherent in the birth struggle of adaptation, which are experienced in coitus, act in a revivifying manner in the same sense as does the nightly regression into sleep. (Ferenczi, 1989, p. 42)

These dangers can bring us to a "renewal", of which philobatic adventures are good examples.

According to Balint, the philobat's phantasy is that the whole world is a loving mother keeping her child in her safe arms. Phylogenetically it is the image of the amorphous sea offering a similarly friendly environment among infinite vistas (Balint, M., 1959, p. 55)

To be overwhelmed by happiness, to enjoy the sight of beauty, to make oneself believe that all is here and nothing is missing—that is the philobat's quest: the oceanic feeling.

The belief in all that elevates mankind—ethics, truth, and freedom—brings us back to the refound harmony of narcissistic completeness.

For those who practise extreme sports, in particular those who flirt with ecstasy and death, the philobat's quest for oceanic feeling belongs to the domain of the art of living rather than to the domain of death. To approach the "oceanic feeling" without being lost and return safely to the base—this is a beautiful project!

Like his successors, Hillary stayed but a few minutes on top of the world; barely having time to entertain a few thoughts about Tibet from above, he shook hands with Tensing Norgay and was already thinking of the even more dangerous way down. After the victory and joy of having been the first, Hillary had to leave the peak and satisfy himself with a medal, a small recognition. He had to return to himself—a re-energised self.

Hillary was barely back in Kathmandu when he learnt of having been knighted by the Queen of England. He recalls, "Stand, Sir Edmund Hillary! Whether I wanted it or not, from now on I was a knight, and was expected to behave like one. What a promotion for a former beekeeper from New Zealand!" (Hillary, 1991). Returning to the safety of one's base to feel the weight of existence, to give up the thrill and undergo a depressive phase once again—this is the risk-taker's ultimate challenge.

Whether in the field of art, science, or thought, progress is set in motion by the conquests of real or metaphorical heights. Conquering these peaks also means struggle with oneself and those things that entrap us and hold us back in body and soul. We advance from one of life's seasons to another struggling, and this necessarily involves separation from those who are dear to us, even if they weigh us down and stand in our way. Within our own time and pace, each of us ultimately take risks, allowing a return to basic safety and settling in this world.

Observing his achievements, Hillary's life can be seen as the creation of a work of art. In *Femmes d'aventure*, I was inspired by Didier Anzieu's work on literary creation and expanded his thought to cover all sorts of creation. Anzieu (1974) distinguishes five stages of creation. I believe that Hillary underwent all five; hence, I will draw my concluding remarks using his example.

1. The root of creation will always be a heroic identification—conscious or unconscious. Hillary remembered a "dreaming phase", fed by his readings. His mind went far away into all sorts of heroic efforts. There was one heroic figure who impressed him very much indeed, the great Antarctic explorer, Shackleton, a tough man and a very good leader. Shackleton had a great ability to inspire his men and lead his team safely out of difficult circumstances. He was a model for Hillary.

    We can also find other heroic identifications in Hillary's story.

2. Inspiration appears to be born out of drives associated with suffering, sadness, and anxiety. It is a matter of harbouring a

latent truth in one's self, which can materialise from the dream to external reality. Such truths are linked to aspects of life and death, questions of origins, and experiences of destabilising crises in our lives. Hillary was only sixteen years old when he started to make the transition between dreaming about adventures and actually pursuing them.

One has to be able to see how the meaning of this truth becomes evident. The new internal order demands that the ocnophile anxiety of change and the philobatic rebelliousness be mastered. Hillary was not to be a beekeeper as was his father before him!

The goal has been set, it became obvious. We could say that Hillary was now able to truly find his way.

Development finds its resources in the world of childhood. The newly found "I" comes to occupy the entire centre stage, and leads to separation from things of lesser value: "All I knew was that I wanted to get involved in adventurous activities. I wanted to do things that were exciting and daring. I had a fairly diffuse feeling as to what precisely they should be" (Hillary, 1991). One who takes the path to creation must embark on a long journey in solitude. He must be careful not to lose himself while flirting with marginalisation, which must be made bearable and controlled. Hillary remembers his teenage years, when he did not have many friends: "I discovered that I tended to be a rather more energetic and stronger walker than the others . . . I loved the outdoors and forcing myself to do lengthy treks—which I enjoyed very much" (Hillary, 1991).

3. In the next phase, the creator must take to heart what he has decided to do, dedicate all his energy to it and maintain a strong will. The whole personality must be involved. It is necessary to become able to apply narcissism within the frames of the task while the superego has to silently perform the job of management and organisation, thus allowing the task at hand to be carried out.

Hillary is thirty-four years old when he joins an Everest reconnaissance expedition, followed by eleven climbs to Himalayan summits. It is −25°C and glacial winds are blowing like "a thousand howling tigers", he describes in his autobiography, *Nothing Venture, Nothing Win* (Hillary, 1975). On 29 May 1953, he launches his offensive with Tensing Norgay. They reach the top.

Four years later, when Balint publishes *Thrills and Regression*, Hillary is back in the Himalayas searching for the Yeti, a "suicide venture" from the scientific point of view, but we have to keep in mind that, after all, he was a dreamer, an adventurer!

4.   In this phase, the creator must let go of the thrill of having touched the stars: he must return to base, back to his ordinary human life.

Hillary remembers this extraordinary moment of achievement, endowing him with instantaneous worldwide fame. According to Anzieu, the creator must be able to return to the ground, break the bubble, and resettle in society. Once again, the superego plays a particularly important role in performing duties like giving speeches, sharing knowledge, and testifying to the experience.

After this stage, Hillary was able to capitalise on his fame and create the Himalaya Trust Foundation, which built schools, hospitals, and bridges in Nepal. Two years later, following Shackleton's footsteps, he conquered new territories in the Antarctic. In 1977, when nearly sixty years old, he explored the Ganges river from its mouth to its source, a distance of over 1200 km.

5.   Finally, says Anzieu, the creator must be able to phrase his message and make it public. Hillary did this with the publication of *High Adventure: The True Story of the First Ascent of Everest* (Hillary, 1955). In the 1960s, he returned to Nepal. Concerned about environmental degradation, he persuaded the Nepalese government to pass laws protecting the forest and declare the area around Everest a National Park. Finally, he used his prestige to convince New Zealand's government to provide financial support to these projects.

The creator's ego should be able to integrate two dimensions of these experiences: the amazement and joy which, according to Anzieu, take us back to the maternal world, and the heroic identification, asceticism, and stoicism, which belong to the world of the father.

Creators are people who bring about formative changes in the way we relate to and see the world. They push the limits of what is possible, of what can be known, while searching for an ideal they can never reach.

Notes

1.   Re-translated from a draft by Etienne Lainé.
2.   The Sherpa are an ethnic group in eastern Nepal.

References

Anzieu, D. (1974). Vers une métapsychologie de la création (Towards a metapsychology of creation). In: *Psychanalyse du génie créateur* (pp. 1–30). Paris: Dunod.

Balint, E. (1959). Distance in space and time. In: M. Balint, *Thrills and Regressions* (pp. 125–131). New York: International Universities Press.

Balint, M. (1959). *Thrills and Regressions*. New York: International Universities Press.

Caillois, R. (1961). *Man, Play and Games*. New York: Free Press of Glencoe.

Cyrulnik, B. (2005). Dialogues. *Clinical Neuroscience, 3*: 217–221.

Ferenczi, S. (1989). *Thalassa: A Theory of Genitality*. London: Karnac.

Hillary, E. (1955). *High Adventure: The True Story of the First Ascent of Everest*. London: Hodder & Stoughton.

Hillary, E. (1975). *Nothing Venture, Nothing Win*. London: Hodder & Stoughton.

Hillary, E. (1991). Interview in Academy of Achievement, Washington, DC. Available at: www.achievement.org/autodoc/page/hil0int-2.

Reverzy, C. (2001). *Femmes d'Aventure: du reve a la Realisation du Soi* (Women of Adventure, the Dream of the Realisation of the Self). Paris: Editions Odile Jacob.

Rousseau, P. (1995). Le deuil périnatal. *Devenir, 7*: 31–60.

CHAPTER NINE

The Enid files

Jennifer Johns

My knowledge of Enid Balint and her style is based primarily on the eight years I spent in analysis with her in the late 1960s and early 1970s. Later, I talked with her, of course (but not nearly enough), and read her papers—both the ones she published with Michael Balint and her own published ones—and the book she was beginning to prepare for publication when she died in 1994 (at the age of ninety).

Michael Parsons, in his introduction to Enid's book, *Before I was I*, writes about his experience of having been in supervision with Enid. He was advised to go to her by his own analyst, who said, "Supervision with Enid is a rather particular sort of experience." Writing about the supervision, Michael felt what he especially gained from her was something about how *to be with* an analytic patient, rather than simply being told how to frame an interpretation or relate what he was observing with theory (though he was told both those things as well). My own experience with her was that of being her patient, and, on reading what Michael had written, I recognised the reciprocal of it: she as my analyst had *been with* me, and though there were interpretations I remembered as having been incisive and accurate, sometimes rather alarmingly so, it had been the "being with", that undoubted

attention and reliable concern for me, that had helped me shed whatever it was that made me so intolerably tense and unforgiving of
myself.

A few weeks ago, I was walking along Marylebone Road, from
Regent's Park Tube station towards Baker Street, and passed Park
Square West, where, at number 7, I had had the majority of my analysis with Enid. I found myself thinking, "I left something there. Something I did not need." After having been slightly anxious and in a
hurry, I found myself relaxing internally, and feeling at once grateful
and sad that the person who had helped me get rid of those particular parts of myself no longer existed. After this, for various reasons, I
found myself wondering for the first time in many years what it was
that I had got from her. I found myself wanting to both answer and
avoid my own questions of what I had got: what identifications, to
what extent I had copied her, what of her might have crept into me,
what valuable aspects of her I had failed to internalise; questions similar to those about what one might or might not have received from
one's parents. One's awareness of the questions bring both pleasure
and displeasure: pleasure that there is someone with whom to iden-
tify (or disidentify), someone to whom one in a way belongs, and
displeasure that one has not in fact invented oneself and there is
someone to whom one owes aspects of oneself—that awful blow to
the remnants of infantile omnipotence. Those thoughts led to others,
particularly in relation to ideas about Ferenczi and the Hungarian
School: how much did this branch of psychoanalytic work influence
Enid's own development as an analyst (and, therefore, indirectly, my
own); how much did she owe to the history and thinking of Budapest,
and how did she make it her own?

Enid was very much her own person. To some, this might seem a
surprise, considering that she shared much of her professional life and
work with someone as powerful and influential as Michael Balint. She
must have spent much of her mental energy thinking with him about
his ideas, and much time on the work they did together at the
Tavistock Clinic, with general practitioners, and with psychosexual
doctors. She had come to this work by her own route, she approached
it in her own way, and, after Michael's death, she continued it in her
own style. There is a clue as to what sort of a person she was long
before she had contact with the psychoanalytic life. The first chapter
of the book she never finished, in which she tries to explain something

Enid Balint, portrait painted by Olga Székely-Kovács.

of her own style, includes a story from her schooldays at an exclusive English girls' boarding school. She explains that she never knew why it was she who was approached by anxious teachers to fetch a fellow pupil who had, on a cold winter's evening, climbed up alone on to the roof. Neither was she certain about why she accepted the task, nor why she behaved as she did when she got there. Not knowing the girl very well, Enid climbed up to the roof and sat down, neither very close to, nor very far from, the girl. She sat quietly, and made no attempt to persuade the girl to come down, but listened as the girl began to talk rapidly and inconsequentially about her family. Enid did not question why the girl was on the roof, but waited until the girl said, spontaneously, that perhaps it was getting too cold to stay there, and Enid then suggested going down.

In repeating this story, I became aware of how often I have reported that certain things were not done, not said, not even under-stood at the time, and perhaps not even later. It is clear, though, that what was somehow known by the young Enid was the importance of calm but attentive listening and waiting. Observation and thought were not absent, but were unobtrusive; there was no apparent urgency to ask or answer questions, but a kind of acceptance that the answers might emerge if necessary.

Until her recollection of this incident late in life, Enid Balint believed that her career as an analyst had arisen out of her work during the Second World War. During the blitz in London she worked with the Family Welfare Association (FWA) organising practical help and advice for distressed and bombed-out civilians. In her work, she found that simply giving information about the availability of government benefits and details of the War Damage Act was often not enough; personal human problems and difficult relationships in marriages and families could be more distressing than loss of home and property, and some civilians had an urgent need to talk about them. She also discovered that, while major events such as fear for one's life, fear of death arriving unexpectedly from the skies, and separation from, or loss of, loved ones were important, many people were more immediately troubled by the apparently minor events in their lives—such as suspicion that someone else was taking their sugar ration or too much of the scarce hot water—and that there was a need to be able to talk about these so-called small things. These realisations led her to set up the Family Discussion Bureau, an offshoot of the FWA, in order to recruit and train others in the work of listening and providing space for understanding, and it was from this that her further professional interests, including psychoanalysis, developed.

After the war, Enid developed links with the newly-formed and exciting Tavistock Institute of Human Relations (TIHR), created by a group of ex-army officers, psychiatrists, psychologists, and sociologists who believed that they could utilise the co-operation they had created and enjoyed during the war and who hoped, so blindly and optimistically, that by expanding their knowledge of human frailties and combining them with psychoanalytic insights, they might help prevent such appalling things from happening again. With the co-operation of such visionaries as Trist, Sutherland, and Wilson, the Family Discussion Bureau became the Institute of Marital Studies within TIHR, still a thriving unit that organises an annual Enid Balint Lecture. It was there that Enid first worked with Michael Balint. Official support from the Home Office was obtained for this training in marital work, and Enid maintained contact with that work until her death.

Enid's own wartime response to human suffering and her recognition of the irrational roots of its causes increased her interest in Freud's thinking: she described Freud's papers as being compulsive reading during those war years. She then trained as a psychoanalyst herself; her first analyst was John Rickman, who had, of course, been an analysand of Ferenczi and Sigmund Freud. Rickman was an extraordinary man; with his special combination of social concern and psychoanalytic understanding, his influence on British psychoanalysis has been quiet, subtle, and deep. He is best known for his ideas on the relationship between the breadth of any field of observation and the theories gathered in that field, and his description of one-body, two-body, three-body, and multi-body psychologies. But his published work (most recently the book edited by Pearl King, 2003) shows his many and varied fields of interest, including something that might be called "psychoanalytical commonsense", and is well worth study. Almost forgotten now, Rickman maintained the place of psychoanalysis in the professional world; he publicised psychoanalytic thinking by organising lectures and publications, and by writing regularly for medical and psychiatric journals. Sadly, Rickman died unexpectedly (while Enid was in analysis with him), ending a career that contributed much to the understanding of object-relations, both in the sense of the relations between internal objects and those between internal and externally perceived objects. After his death, Enid became the analysand of Donald Winnicott, whose thinking she engaged with and related to, and whose ideas she used, but with whom she did not always agree (as she had not always agreed with Michael Balint). Another link with Ferenczi was through her supervision with Melanie Klein, which she valued. Michael Balint's thinking and development of Ferenczi's ideas was also inevitably an important part of her life—important for both her individual clinical psychoanalytic work and her role as Michael's partner in the work that he started with general practitioners, psychiatrists, medical students, and psychosexual doctors.

After Balint's death in 1971 (the same year her second analyst, Winnicott, died), Enid continued their joint work, travelling internationally to many centres for seminars to lecture and supervise seminar leaders in what had become known as Balint Groups. Although not medically trained, she strongly supported doctors and their psychoanalytic training, as well as the use of psychoanalytic thinking in medicine; she believed that psychoanalysis must keep in contact with the patient as a whole person, with a body that brings the patient, and communicates with the analyst. However, she was not teaching psychoanalysis to GPs, certainly not encouraging interpretation that might lead to a different kind of transference to that which normally occurs between doctor and patient, but discovering that the understanding of the relationship between doctor and patient was often enough in itself to facilitate change, without verbal clarification.

Indeed, Enid was interested in preverbal, non-verbal and unconscious communication, as well as perception, imagination, and creativity. Timing, and the awareness that premature interpretation can be damaging, was a hallmark of her individual clinical work.

For those of you who would like to know her better, I can recommend her book, *Before I was I*, published by Free Association Books shortly before she died, and edited by Juliet Mitchell and Michael Parsons. It contains her main psychoanalytic papers, supplemented by papers about her work with GPs and with marital therapists. Her papers describe her better than I can. Clinical description is delicate and sensitive. She wrote about such matters as the analyst's field of observation; she insisted that there be a clear difference between observation and the inferences that might be drawn from it, and the importance of those things that might be missed when the observing process is hindered by the analyst's adherence to known theory. She writes about the sense of self emerging from the earliest relationship, when the mother can respond to the child in such a way that the child can know it has been recognised, and calls this "feed-back".

Commenting on Freud's metaphor of the mirror-analyst, she warns against the temptation for the analyst to abandon the strictly analytic technique of listening for associations for the more "kindly" one of friendliness and warmth, which could leave the ill, needy part of the patient unrecognised and abandoned. There is further elaboration of her thoughts about dynamic mutuality of experience and the capacity for recognition (that Balint also calls "echoing") in a paper called "Fair shares and mutual concern", which addresses both early experiences and methods of child care and develops ideas about educational styles and theories. Other papers describe a variety of patients: a patient whose life was superficially successful, whose analysis revealed an area of absence of language and memory in relation to a reality found unbearable and disavowed in infancy;

potentially creative patients living in a subjectively empty world experienced patchy early recognition; a woman who became panic-stricken at any loss and could not tolerate any separation from her baby was affected unconsciously by her own mother's unrecognised separation from her natural mother, the patient's grandmother.

Her writing about her marital work and the seminars for GPs also include her thinking about unconscious communication and the importance of understanding relationships. Her insistence that evidence be picked up carefully and in detail, that conclusions not be quickly jumped to, that observation include both an identification with a patient's experience and an ability to stand outside and view the problem from outside—the "biphasic" position—echoes her attitude in the consulting room.

Enid was an active training analyst of the British Psychoanalytical Society and was a major influence in the training scheme, at both an organisational and a teaching level. Although clear in her own ideas, she was not partisan in the aftermath of the Controversial Discussions that threatened the integrity of the British Society, and she had a great respect for the work of individual analysts from all sections of the Society. She was consulted by many colleagues, from all schools, as being fair-minded and open, and was generous in her listening.

Her place in the psychoanalytic firmament is an interesting one. In terms of psychoanalytic genealogy, she descends from Freud via Rickman (and less directly via Winnicott, who was analysed by Strachey), and from Ferenczi and the Hungarian tradition via, again, Rickman, with Balint added in; this background, together with more than a little respect for Klein's thinking, creates a recipe for a unique position. Enid Balint's own gifts, already available to her by the age of thirteen, and certainly visible to her schoolteachers, underlie these later influences, which gave rise to her own voice. To end, I would like to quote some of Enid's own words, as spoken to another analysand, Juliet Mitchell, about her own way of analysing.

> The small thing that the patient tells the analyst is probably not in itself what matters, but what matters is not some big thing either. What the small thing leads to may be some other very small thing, perhaps from the past. What often happens in analytic work is that the patient brings something about the neighbour smelling horrible, or something nasty in this particular room this morning; who has been there perhaps. You listen. You don't say anything then; you don't

Dr Michael Balint and Mrs Enid Balint, by Olga Dormandi (sister of Alice Balint).

make an interpretation which turns it into something important, about the smell of a mother, or whatever. If you do that, you may be neglecting and misunderstanding the patient by understanding too quickly. You have to wait and see what it is about, and perhaps you find it is about a smell when the child was small, or perhaps something quite different. You don't know to begin with, but if you come in too soon with an interpretation, you might miss a dream, for example, by interrupting the flow of association. In my view it's much easier if you have an association, then maybe a dream, then more associations; and then you get back to the bad smell at the beginning. But if you come in too soon, you are doing what I am anxious about at the moment, both in general practice but more so, much more so, in analysis, which is that people may hang on to set-piece interpretation. I think we have given up the idea of its being all the Oedipus complex, or all parental neglect, or all anything. We get tiny little important details which really make things alive for the patient, and then, once you do that, the patient tells you something different and unexpected. That is the transference in the true sense.

Bibliography

Balint, E. The girl on the roof, or Listening to strangers (unfinished and unpublished).

Balint, E. (1993). *Before I was I: Psychoanalysis and the Imagination*. London. Free Association Books.

Balint, E., & Norell, J. S. (2001). *Six Minutes for the Patient: Interactions in General Practice Consultation*. London: Routledge.

Balint, E., Courtenay, M., Elder, A., Hull, S., & Juli, P. (1993). *The Doctor, The Patient and The Group: Balint Revisited.* London: Routledge.

King, P. (2003). *No Ordinary Psychoanalyst: The Exceptional Contributions of John Rickman* London: Karnac.

PART IV
CLOSER TO OUR TIME

CHAPTER TEN

Survival strategies:
a psychoanalytic view

Judit Szekacs-Weisz

> "Being alone leads to splitting. The presence of someone with whom one can share and communicate joy and sorrow (love and understanding) can heal the trauma"
>
> (Ferenczi, 1988, p. 200)

Hungarians are professional survivors. No wonder they are; history made them learn the arts-and-crafts of survival.

To understand an essential feature of "East-European existence", one has to recognise the fact that in this part of the world historic changes did not leave much time for psychodynamic working through. Dramatic events, elementary changes in the perception of values, functions and social roles came in a rapid flow. Whole nations and generations lived under the influence of cumulative traumatisation.

After the Second World War, new concepts of state, establishment, organisation, institute and executive bodies emerged in these countries. The structure and functions of the totalitarian state determined human conditions, existence, and relationship in professional, official, and private areas. Adaptation to the conflict-ridden power structure and realisation of contradictory interests raised many basic questions concerning the development of individual and group identity. This is why I suggest that when we look at Eastern Europe, no psychodynamic study analysing possible reactions to, or consequences of, social traumata can be meaningful or valid unless it is done through the prism of historic transformations.

These countries offer a lot to learn about overt and hidden mechanisms governing human conditions in totalitarian states. Collecting more information, analysing these processes at work can provide evidence that would enable us to rethink our psychoanalytical understanding of the nature of social traumatisation and the mechanisms of survival. This work started in the last decade; however, it is still in an early phase. In order to arrive at a more complete insight into the mental and emotional picture of the twentieth century human drama—I am convinced—this work needs to be continued.

This chapter is about clinical experiences, social phenomena, and ideas of linkages between them.

Pychodynamic phenomena related to survival mechanisms captured my attention at the end of the 1970s.This was a period in Hungary when the dictatorship targeting the mind became considerably milder and psychoanalytic thinking was possible on a broader scale again. I was working in one of the biggest teaching hospitals in Budapest and also in private practice, so I had the chance to meet quite a number of young adults. Some of them applied for psychoanalysis; others were referred to me for analytical psychotherapy.

Working with them made me gradually aware of a set of specific psychodynamic phenomena that I found characteristic of this postwar "second generation". (The fact that I also belong to this generation had its advantages in seeing certain connections, but, at the same time, it called for handling the material with extra care and intensive working through.) For many years, it seemed quite unlikely that my observations could ever be published, so I kept writing notes for my desk, referring to these patients in them as "Children of the Iron Curtain".

In the consulting room, the first apparent feature to perceive was that these young men and women have been struggling with severe conflicts of identification and identity. Lack of continuity in experiencing time and space characterised the clinical picture. Flexible boundaries of the body and ego had not developed; these boundaries proved unstable, fragile, and penetrable. Primitive mechanisms of defence prevailed. Fragmentation, splitting and idealisation and projective identification were dominant.

Answering the question "what is 'trauma'?", Ferenczi, in whose life the concept of trauma has always occupied a central position,[1] writes in his *Diary* in 1932,

> 'Concussion,' reaction to an 'unbearable' external or internal stimulus in an autoplastic manner (modifying the self) instead of an alloplastic manner (modifying the stimulus). A neoformation of the self is impossible without the previous destruction, either partial or total, or dissolution of the former self. A new ego cannot be formed directly from the previous ego, but from fragments, more or less elementary products of its disintegration (splitting, atomisation). The relative strength of the 'unbearable' excitation determines the degree and depth of the ego's disintegration . . . (Ferenczi, 1988[1932], p. 181)

Ferenczi's description of the trauma and resulting disorders in the formation of the ego brings the striking features of the clinical picture back to our mind. Indeed, when we look at my patients' history, we find that they have all suffered different degrees of multiple traumatisation.

There was the idyllic world, which they believed in, but which never existed, except in words, wishes, and phantasies, and there existed the real world present in their experiences, though acknowledging it and talking about it has never been approved of. Such an unresolvable conflict results in fragmented mental functions.

In Suzy's case, this took the form of pseudostupidity; her cognitive functions were severely impaired. By her adolescent years, this intelligent and bright girl was not able to perceive the meaning of words, see connections, and orientate in situations and tasks. Teachers and friends alike believed that she was slow, clumsy, and disorganised.

For her the world could not become the source of learning. Learning and experience had to be kept rigorously apart, or else the integrity of her psychic world would be threatened by chaos and breakdown. Splitting and fragmentation accompanied by idealisation and denial become the most powerful means of psychic defence.

Suzy's material is a plastic illustration of the most characteristic mental dysfunction of this generation, which I will refer to as *the principle of splitting and fragmentation*. Putting these archaic mechanisms of defence in the service of preserving psychic integrity appears to function as a most powerful and effective strategy of mental survival. This corresponds to the collective experience of the citizens in a totalitarian state, which make them accept that facts and ideas exist separately.

In the process of splitting and keeping apart learning and experience, a determinant model of the Soviet regime is observed: practice and ideology are separated and principles define the perception and testing of reality. Fragmentation rules the dimension of time, as well. Fragmented time provides the frame for the mental apparatus to work through fragmented psychic experiences. Psychic reality is constructed of isolated bits. Both reality testing and memory are impaired. Phantasy and reality are easily confused, on both societal and individual levels.

Totalitarian systems exploit these effects of social traumatisation and also actively create such dysfunctions in the human mind. These are put in the service of the regime: often they are declared as desirable norms and depicted as attributes of progressive thinking and development.[2]

The post-war generation inherited and was born into this texture of never-elaborated multi-generational experiences. Their parents fell victim both to the Holocaust and to the Soviet system; therefore, their children are the *second generation* in a multiple sense.

Many of them were of Jewish origin on one or both sides. They were children of Holocaust victims: the second generation. However powerful this classification is in itself, it fails to describe basic aspects of their life history and development. What is decisive in their case is that their parents, unlike many of their fellow survivors, did not emigrate from the country of their persecution; actually, a great number of those deported returned "home" from the camps to start life anew. For them, the vicissitudes of elaborating those extreme experiences that shattered their basic trust in human existence were determined by this fact. Very soon, history intervened in their lives again: in 1948, a totalitarian communist regime took power in Hungary. The illusion of a possibly democratic development and stabilisation faded away and the country was set behind the "iron curtain", that expressive symbol of isolation and dictatorship.

Kate's story could be a kind of East European "cliché". Suzy's mother is the only surviving member of a rich upper-middle-class Jewish family. Her parents and two brothers perished in concentration camps. Her father comes from a little village. The smart peasant boy is lifted by the movements of the new era. Like a number of talented sons and daughters of agricultural and industrial workers, he is offered a place at one of the best universities. The "shiny winds"[3] (a popular symbol of these early, formative years taken from the lyrics of a contemporary march) blew the couple together. Promises and illusions of a new, just, and more complete life, party meetings, mass actions organised to speed up the rebuilding of the country, laid the common ground for their life together. This shared area becomes especially important for them, as it is meant to balance the fact that they arrive from social worlds, values, principles, and behavioural patterns so far apart. These activities create a powerful illusion of belonging, which blurs their perception of basic contradictions and conflicts for many years to come. The resulting mythology registers only the idyllic features of their family life. A kind of tribal existence develops. Their closed world is reinforced by the hardships and dramatic events of the 1950s. So much so that when the world starts to change around them a few years later, this family proves resistant to the transformations in the world outside. The motionlessness is partly due to the fact that frightening aspects of their inner world have always been split off and projected outside. This way, the world could be kept hostile and persecutory. Going outside meant danger. Reality testing becomes practically impossible for the members of this family, especially the children. Overtones of heroic pathos obscured the almost unbearable reality: poverty, multiple co-tenancy (they shared a flat with three other families), and professional humiliations combined with desperate arguments and physical violence at home.

Family secrets related to both present and past increase their isolation. The structure of the family becomes more and more rigid. These distortions interfere with their chances of integrating fragmented parts and aspects.

Under such circumstances, different groups (ethnic, professional, religious, etc.) elaborate guidelines for their members, which define the area of acceptable compromises in adapting their basic human perspectives to the confines and boundaries prescribed by the system. The guidelines must be flexible, since these boundaries are subject to change according to the momentary political interests and aims. It is essential for all strata of society to find the rules that are likely to secure their physical and psychic survival.

Some of these rules express vital principles of adjustment, so that gradually they are accepted by the majority of the subjects. They are so powerful that I feel justified in calling them the *Commandments of survival*.

In Hungary, the greatest part of the population accepted the *Commandment of mediocrity*.

One has to realise that anything beyond central control is experienced by a totalitarian system as potentially dangerous. Maybe the most painful lesson to be learnt from such a regime is that individuality is suspicious, sticking out is bravado, and can sometimes cost one's life. Individual plans and ideas are not permitted. The man who tries to bridge the gap between distant parts of reality often questions the centrally approved version of truth. This is how talent and creativity acquire pejorative connotations: these faculties become synonyms of maladaptation. To think anew or to create anew is dangerous; he who follows the commandment of mediocrity has better chances of survival and assimilation.

In many families, where the 1950s smashed the career of the young parents (be they artisans, businessmen, or well-to-do peasants), another commandment was formulated, genetically related to the previous one. The message of this commandment towards the second generation was: do not be successful!

Agnes, twenty-seven, came to see me because she was unable to complete her thesis. Dates for its submission were postponed, one after the other. She was very concerned about these "surprising" difficulties, since she, as a rule, was able to write easily and work fast with good results. Her subject was related to the history of one of the leading literary journals in Hungary.

As the story of her life unfolds, I learn about her parents, who were talented young journalists. Through the "shiny winds" period, they worked for different prestigious papers. During the course of the Rajk Trial (the first of the show trials *à la* Moscow) they were investigated, and though they were not actually imprisoned, the shadow of suspicion was cast over them, so that they lost their jobs and the right of publication under their own names. They were forced to the periphery of their profession for the next decade. As they were under *silencium* (prohibition of publication), they wrote for their desk drawers or made translations under borrowed names for several years to come.

It took nearly a year to arrive at an understanding of the unconscious paradox Agnes had been obeying. For her to become successful in creating a valuable piece of writing and making it officially accepted was impossible, as unconsciously it meant disloyalty to the image of her parents. Under the pressure of this dilemma she came to face basic questions related to her identity, and also to the world around her. Escorting Agnes on this difficult journey in the psychic reality of her family history, understanding and interpreting split off and suppressed aspects of its social dimensions, created a chance to submit her childhood fears and inherited bogeys to reality testing in the light of her own experiences. Once we were able to work this material through, as part and parcel of this process, the dissertation could also be completed.

During periods of rapid and massive change in the social system (which is, more often than not, experienced as a crisis), principles of survival mechanisms become activated and, therefore, they are more visible and obvious.

Let us quote Ferenczi again:

> Possibly complicated mechanisms (living beings) can only be preserved as units by the pressure of their environment. At an unfavourable change in the environment the mechanism falls to pieces and disintegrates as far (probably along the lines of antecedent historic development) as the greater simplicity and consequent plasticity of the elements makes a new adaptation possible. (Ferenczi, 1955, p. 220)

How far does one have to go back? It seems at least to the period of the previous traumatisation, sometimes much further, to the time of another trauma which has been elaborated well enough to enable it to be assessed by the present generations as a positive change. Maybe this is how the Hungarian Holy Crown of the eleventh century (a symbol of Christianity, feudalism, and progress in medieval times) was chosen to be placed on top of the new national coat-of-arms at the end of the 1990s. The coat-of-arms was to symbolise the new, post-Communist Hungary. Profound changes following the collapse of the Berlin Wall in 1989 brought the participant observer to revelations concerning phenomena related to the return of the repressed in mass psychology. Mental and ideological ghosts of the Second World War came to life in the public sphere. Unfreezing of these systems released signs, symbols, concepts, values, beliefs, and ideologies in their original, unchanged form. They reflect the way they had been frozen as a consequence of the unresolved dynamics of the previous social metamorphosis. Anachronistic, primitive, sometimes monstrous, elements, which belong to a distant past that is hardly known by the younger generations, are melted out.

Given favourable conditions, they could be put in the service of working through of social traumata, so that the continuity of being could be re-established. If the change is rapid, there is no time for elaboration, therefore more democratic means cannot be developed. The new leaders in power will want to control what is in the citizen's mind no less than the previous ones.

In this way, uncontrolled memories will not be welcome; a few of the "unfrozen memories" will be selected and become sanctioned. These will serve political–ideological aspirations. The main function of these memories in such constellations is to cover up memories that are alive, which people could recall, memories of their own experience, feelings, roles, acts, attachments, and reservations; memories of collective and individual experience, which could provide a source of learning and would act against splitting and fragmentation.

In the name of freedom, a new cycle of totalitarian mind control is born. This leads us to the next commandment, which states: Do not remember!

We see how memories can become dangerous. Where the continuity of being is interrupted over and over again, the identity of the people becomes conditional and fragmented, as well. Remembering previous identities, acts, behaviour, or thoughts might be felt as a dangerous provocation, as if a relevant proportion of the people in power would really expect that the others believe what they state: that is, that from a given point in time everything happened the other way round. (George Orwell described this phenomenon as early as the 1940s.) Remembrance is linked with shame and secrets, not only individual and family secrets, but also secrets of larger units, groups, sometimes whole nations.

Exploring functions linked to memories in new social formations (as in Eastern Europe) offers a chance to study how such functions (remembering and forgetting) can fall victim to outer control. These observations also call for the analysis of the mechanisms that result in the impairment of memory as a consequence of accumulated social traumata. The role that "commanded forgetting", "remembering", and repression play in the elaboration and/or perpetuation of the social trauma also needs reconsideration. A system that is unable to allow for remembrance is governed by rigid control. This will foster repetition, not change.

In his trauma concept, Ferenczi finds it theoretically important that

> . . . 3) no memory traces of such impressions remain, even in the unconscious, and thus the causes of the trauma can not be recalled from memory traces. If, in spite of it, one wants to reach them, which logically appears to be almost impossible, then one must repeat the trauma itself and under more favourable conditions one must bring it for the first time to perception and to motor discharge. (Ferenczi, 1955, p. 240)

One observes such repetitions in the course of both individual experiences and historical events. Sometimes, they present themselves in a well-defined set or sequence. Often, these sequences are so coherent that they create the impression of following a hidden script.

In Hungary, as a first visible sign of a massive social change, the middle section of national flags were cut out so that they could get rid of the previous regime's coat-of-arms in the centre. Several former East European countries followed this tradition. The next step was to change the names of streets. In Budapest, all the names that had anything to do with the previous regime were crossed out and new plates were fixed next to them. This phase was followed by the removal of statues and other relics, such as the red stars.

This sequence has been repeated in Hungary three times during the five decades after the Second World War: in 1945, in 1956, and after 1989. (Today, as a new edition of attacks on linking, we witness a powerful wave of attempts at rewriting history and destroying collective knowledge and memories of shared experience of the recent and more distant past.) The overwhelming urge to demolish the symbols of totalitarian regimes expresses the wish of an instant separation from the values of the previous era.

Sometimes, this process mobilises very primitive mechanisms of destruction, like those at work in 1956, when the statue of Stalin was pulled down in Budapest. Thousands of people took part in chopping the statue into little pieces, so that everybody could take a fragment home, possibly to preserve a piece of the whole, but also to make sure that it could never be put together again. To prevent destruction in a critical moment in 1990 (proving that the historical script was widely familiar), Lenin's statue erected on the very place had been removed by the government "due to metal fatigue". The city was greatly amused.

We have been discussing psychodynamic processes that are embedded in socio-historical transformations. These processes have direct effects on the development of individual and group identity. They are also responsible for specific modifications in the perception of, and the reactions to, social expectations and requirements. Professional and urban jargon alike calls them the *strategies of survival*.

I believe that if we apply Byng-Hall's concept of the family script to the social sphere, we find a very useful tool for understanding the dynamics of survival strategies. He writes,

> Scripts which avoid catastrophic interaction are necessary for the stability of the family. Families need safe scripts. At times, however it seems clear to an observer that the beliefs about what is happening is not the whole story. It is a myth. Myths distort the truth in order to create a defence. Ferreira (1963) described family myths as providing a blueprint for action. There is a good case for separating out the blueprint function of the myth and calling it a family script. (Byng-Hall, 1985, p. 304)

In my definition, survival strategies are scripts describing and conveying possible modes of escape from extreme circumstances and threatening situations of crisis. They are formulated through personal experiences of the generations surviving the danger. They contain elements of both external and internal reality, synthesising conscious and unconscious aspects of the critical situation. They encapsulate information of vital importance. Survival strategies train the inexperienced how to be alert, they sharpen the skills for recognising danger and the possible resources of help. They provide a blueprint for action, regulate the sequence of orientation, and prepare for economic, fast reactions. They function as unchallengeable psychological axioms. They also ensure that these skills are not forgotten.

From this aspect, they function as some kind of auxiliary multigenerational memory traces. Carrying essential directives, survival strategies are handed carefully over to the next generation, most often by means of family legends and myths.

Judit was a young doctor in a teaching hospital. Her professor suggested she sought professional help to "sort out her scandalous behaviour", which upset the discipline at the department and made it questionable whether she could keep her job. The story that unfolded was as follows. Due to changes in the military policy of the country, it was announced that female medical staff were also to be drafted for professional service. Women were required to report at the military base to fill in forms and take tests. It did not worry the other members of the staff too much; they thought it was just another formality and did not pay too much attention to the matter. Judit vehemently opposed the whole idea from the first moment and flatly refused to go. She tore up one official letter after the other and announced to her flabbergasted colleagues that if she did not find understanding from the management she would leave the hospital, or even the whole medical field, rather than obey this order. Her colleagues became very concerned, as they liked the well-qualified, responsible young woman, and anxiously pushed Judit to find her way to my consulting room. After a series of vehement outbursts against the absurdity of the system that tolerated such "idiotic measures", she gave me the clue to her conflict. During the war, Judit's uncle, a famous neurologist, was killed in one of the forced labour battalions in Ukraine set up for Jews. Her father, also a doctor, decided not to obey the draft order, and escaped by producing false papers. This saved his life. He went into hiding and survived. Judit was told this story over and over again, until she learnt her lesson. No wonder, when a situation faintly resembling the phantasised one arose, she immediately "knew" what to do. She did have a rational understanding of the actual situation and saw why her colleagues thought her behaviour was "out of proportion", but the power of the inner command was so strong that she was unable to question the nature of the situation, weigh the risks involved, and modify her reactions. Any suggestion of departure from her survival script provoked such intense anxieties that the tentative attempts at reality testing had immediately to be given up. In this case, the social changes were faster than the therapeutic working through. Just about when we became able to see these connections more clearly, the whole Ministry of Defence was reorganised and the project of drafting women duly criticised and abandoned. In the course of our work, Judit decided to start analysis with me and stayed on for another four years.

Conceptualising the nature of survival strategies along these lines has theoretical and methodological implications to our therapeutic work: this approach calls for a simultaneous testing of external and psychic reality. It uses a multi-generational model that enables us to trace the material back to its origins in space and time. Introducing the concept of "script" creates a workable technical and theoretical frame for psychodynamic understanding of actual social systems.

The most relevant methodological consequence drawn from analyses of these survival scripts is that working through these powerful blueprints in the mind seems to be a basic condition for opening up the personal domain of traumatic experiences through which one might find the way to the elaboration of the trauma.

Returning to the social stage, observing the effects of traumatic social changes in our time, it feels painfully actual and, at the same time, illuminating to quote Schönberger-Szekacs's analysis of ego disorders resulting from the extreme experience of war. The survivor's original and sensitive words recall some of Ferenczi's revelations.

> ... the effect of the immense quantity of hatred and destruction accompanying war will cause depersonalisation, in consequence of which the "peace" ego gets lost; in the process of adaptation to these traumatic circumstances a new "war" ego will come into existence. Whatever favours the feeling of reconstructive omnipotence will render it possible for the "war" ego to form a new "peace" ego. This will restore healthy equilibrium, and this is the psychological significance of reconstruction. But this equilibrium is necessarily different from what it was before. A trauma that has once taken place cannot be undone by any reconstruction, though the feeling of reconstructive omnipotence accompanying acts of physical reconstruction may give the individual and the community an increased self-confidence. A common trauma and a common collective recovery, i.e. reconstruction, will produce new egos which will necessarily differ from the egos of those who had undergone either the trauma or the recovery. (Schönberger-Szekacs, 1948, p. 248)

Circumstances which interrupt the continuity of the elaboration of social traumata make the formation of this "peace" ego conditional.

When society changes too dramatically and/or too fast, integrating experiences of the previous phase is not possible. Testing the validity of the "inherited" survival strategies is extremely difficult.

Instability increases the power of survival scripts. They become more rigid and, through this, they lose their capacity to mobilise prompt and adequate reactions. Instead, they tend to impair the perception of real situations and conditions, thus hindering flexible adaptation and reality testing. In such constellations, transformations in the outside world are experienced as chaos and change becomes a source of alarm.

Studying survival strategies and commandments of different social configurations is a meaningful task that takes us far beyond the confines of our consulting rooms. Not only can they help us achieve a more profound understanding of our patients, but also, in the "here and now" of historic processes, they contribute to a more dynamic insight into the decisive formative factors of a given era. Illuminating collective and individual aspects in the elaboration of social traumatisation, they can also improve our vision of the possible forces that play a role in the creation of a social atmosphere where continuity of experience is safeguarded and where basic aspects of identity formation can be rediscovered.

Notes

1. Besides personal and strictly scientific reasons, one can postulate that this involvement is due to the fact that he was born in Hungary, and lived his whole life in this small "occupation prone" country that has a history of subordination and dependence over the past 400 years. Understanding the world around, therefore, has been a vital task for individual and societal survival for the successive generations. No wonder the idea of external reality is never absent from Ferenczi's conceptualisations.

2. Individual and societal traumatisation go hand-in-hand. Similar processes can be observed in the genesis and effects of the trauma and the various attempts at its elaboration on both levels. Nevertheless, phenomenological analogies have to be investigated so that the specific dynamic differences could clearly unfold. Falling into the trap of forcing principles of individual dynamics on mass psychology and vice versa would lead to a distorted trauma theory.

3. "Hey, our flags by shiny winds are blown / Hey, there are words on it: long live freedom / Winds, oh shiny winds blow, just blow! / We'll turn the world over by tomorrow".

References

Byng-Hall, J. (1985). The family script: a useful bridge between theory and practice. *Journal of Family Therapy*, 7(3): 301–305.

Ferenczi, S. (1955). *Final Contributions to the Problems and Methods of Psycho-Analysis*, M. Balint (Ed.), E. Mosbacher & others (Trans.). London: Hogarth Press [reprinted, London: Karnac, 1994].

Ferenczi, S. (1988)[1932]. *The Clinical Diary of Sándor Ferenczi*, J. Dupont (Ed.), M. Balint & N. Z. Jackson (Trans.). Cambridge, MA: Harvard University Press.

Ferreira, J. (1963). Family myth and homeostasis. *Archives of General Psychiatry*, 9: 457–463.

Székács-Schönberger, I. (1948). Disorders of the ego in wartime. *British Journal of Medical Psychology*, 21(4): 248–253.

CHAPTER ELEVEN

"In more favourable circumstances": ambassadors of the wound[1]

Rachel Rosenblum (pour Henri Danon Boileau)

This chapter starts with an empirical question. Why is it so dangerous for survivors of major traumas to tell their story? Why do they often pay the price of telling the "ghastly tale" by committing suicide? Look at Jean Amery, Primo Levi, Paul Celan, Piotr Rawicz; look also at more ambiguous cases like those of Romain Gary, Georges Perec (illness), G. Sebald (accident). What do these writers share besides the intensity of their traumatisation and the decision to confront their past? What are the gestures that increase the dangers inherent in addressing past traumas? Are there safeguards against such dangers?

Those who return to past traumas often succeed in not returning alone. Sometimes, they return with psychoanalysts as travelling companions. Sometimes, they do so with companions they had never actually met, but encountered in literature, philosophy, or art. In the first case, facing the past trauma might become a shared experience. In the second case, the experience might also be shared, but indirectly: it takes place via *screen texts*, narratives of the traumas endured by others. In the first case, the sharing occurs in the same physical space, in the same room. In the second case, the sharing is distant, oblique. In both cases, companions act as "ambassadors" in charge of connecting victims to their wounded self, making it easier for trauma victims to address an unbearable past. Thus, some psychoanalysts became "ambassadors" of the wound, companions of the trauma victims. Was it their role? If not so, what should be their role?

Key concepts will be guiding this exploration. These concepts come largely from the work of Sandor Ferenczi, and from the "realist" approach to trauma he defended at great risk during the last years of his life when he challenged "an overestimation of the phantasy dimension, and . . . the underestimation of traumatic reality in the pathogenesis" (Ferenczi, 1929, p. 374). Ferenczi's approach proved quite relevant when, in the 1970s, survivors of the horrors of the Second World War started to address their traumatic experiences. Analysts in a number of countries needed a perspective that would account for historically attested traumas, a theoretical construct that would go beyond a much too exclusive stress on phantasising. Ferenczi's writings provided them with such a construct.

Particularly important for the purpose of this chapter is a series of notes written between 1929 and 1932. Often, these notes are extraordinarily concise. Sometimes, they need to be "unpacked'. Each word counts. Every sentence leads to a research programme. From these notes, I would like to cull three major ideas.

The first idea expresses Ferenczi's return to a certain amount of "realism". Ferenczi stresses the tendency of trauma victims to doubt or disbelieve their own experience. For such patients the doubt, whether reality or phantasy, remains, even though everything points to reality. Often, such patients would rather consider their memory unreliable than believe that such things can happen. In a way, they proceed to the self-sacrifice of the integrity of their mind. This sacrifice provides them with an escape (Ferenczi, 1932, p. 106).

I propose to summarise the second idea by referring to two brief fragments from Ferenczi's paper, written in December 1932, but published posthumously. In the first, Ferenczi suggests that repetition in analysis is worse than original trauma. In the second, he notes that psychoanalysis is often the site in which the traumatic experience must become perceptible for the first time (Ferenczi, 1934).

Ferenczi notes that the brutality of a traumatic experience could entail much worse consequences than disowning it or disbelieving it. It might act like "an anaesthetic, interrupting all psychic activity, triggering a state of passivity, an absence of resistance" (Ferenczi, 1934).

This may entail an erasure of the event, or at least a loss of affect that explains the apparent indifference of trauma victims when they report on tragic experiences; a loss that leads to the puzzlement of analysts when they seem the only ones to show emotion (Chasseguet-Smirgel, 2000; Rosenblum, 2009). What subsists of the traumatic event is an empty shell . . . "The victim's narrative . . . testifies to an absence, to an event that has not yet come into existence, in spite of the compelling and overwhelming nature of the reality of its occurrence" (Laub, 1992a, p. 57). This means that a traumatic event often remains dormant, until it becomes "perceptible for the first time" in the context of therapy. This "postponed" first time might indeed be "worse" than the original occurrence, since pain is now summoned in full consciousness.

Ferenczi's third major point concerns the conditions in which the repeat of the event must be performed. He maintained that if you want to reach the origin of an unexpected shock, one that is sudden and overwhelming, the trauma itself must be repeated in more favourable circumstances. It must become perceptible for the first time. I have already discussed the issue of "repeating" and the question of the "first time". What I wish to stress now is the way in which the trauma must be repeated. Ferenczi's words are "in more favourable circumstances". What are such "more favourable circumstances"?

Are there "more favourable circumstances" that explain why there are comparatively fewer suicides among trauma survivors who did not write their stories? Is therapy always able to provide "more favourable circumstances"? If not, when does it, and why?

The suffocating air of writing

The great catastrophes of history can be recognised through the paralysed silence they leave in their wake, a silence that is frequently broken only to make way for the falsifications of memory. Between silence and falsification, a third path may be opened. For those who are capable of it, this path involves saying what happened, writing in the first person. This third possibility is that of public testimony. It allows an unspeakable truth to erupt on to the social scene, hopefully with a cathartic function. The author of the testimony would, in this way, be unburdening himself or herself of a horror too heavy to bear. Once put into words, suffering would be shared. It is the virtue of such a sharing whose power to grant peace is debated here. Apart from the fact that it is accessible only to subjects capable of putting their experience in words, the path of writing might prove perilous. One can choke on the fact that certain things have never been said. But one can also suffer from the fact that they have been "badly" said, "badly" heard, "badly" received. There would be good and bad ways of testifying, good and bad interlocutors, writings which save you and writings which prove risky. One could go one step further and suggest that witnesses might suffer from the mere fact that certain things were uttered at all. The very process of remembering them can, in many instances, be lethal. Instead of ridding their authors of the horror, some texts do nothing but hurl them headlong into it.

Of course, one can deny the existence of a direct relation between the process in the course of which a certain number of unbearable feelings came into the public domain and the death of those who felt and expressed those feelings. Yet, a doubt remains. For example, one may wonder why the poet Paul Celan took his own life. When it was a question of speaking about Auschwitz, he was the only one, says George Steiner, who was not at a loss for words. Paul Celan found the right words and he found them in the language of the murderers. Yet, despite (or because of) having found these words, Paul Celan committed suicide in Paris in 1970, at the height of his powers, victim of "overwhelming desolation". What did this "overwhelming desolation" consist of?

Several writers who returned from deportation tried to answer the question. Jorge Semprun is quite explicit about the deadly power of writing. Certain themes, he warns, cannot be embarked upon with impunity. As he remarks in a book significantly entitled *Literature or Life* (1994), there are times when a choice has to be made, to live or to write. A choice has to be made between the

> murmuring silence of life and the "murderous" exercise of writing
> ... Writing plunged me back into death, submerged me in it. I was
> choking on the suffocating air of my drafts. I failed in my attempt to
> say death so as to reduce it to silence. If I had continued, it would
> probably have been death which would have silenced me ... (1994,
> p. 235)

Semprun opted for "voluntary amnesia"; he made the choice of "becoming an other in order to remain oneself", of changing his topic in order to remain alive. He would not recount the horror "except at excessive cost, at the cost of my own survival, in a manner of speaking, since writing ceaselessly leads me back into the aridity of a deathly experience . . ."

In fact, Semprun managed to write and also to survive. Does this mean that, in some cases, one can speak the catastrophe without being once again caught in it? It might depend on whether or not the narrative of their trauma induces guilt, or worse—shame. Not all traumas are associated with shame. Some involve the pride of resisting an inflicted wound. Semprun—who was sent to a concentration camp and not to an extermination camp—was deported as a resistant. His status was that of a political prisoner. His pride makes a huge difference. Yet, how does one speak the catastrophe? And to whom? In other words, are there "good narratives", narratives that a person can tell and yet survive?[2]

These questions are addressed to every one of us, but particularly to psychoanalysts, for it falls to psychoanalysts to modulate speech through listening, to preserve the possibility of an elaboration in the face of horror. In order to better understand the conditions in which such an elaboration is possible, or ceases being so, let us turn to a powerful example: let us examine the life and death of a French philosopher, Sarah Kofman.

Kofman's experience is exemplary, not merely because of her brilliant mind, but by the number of registers she relied on when it came to confronting the intensity of her suffering. As an essayist, Kofman offered a series of " oblique" narratives. As a patient, she recorded and discussed the successes and shortcomings of her own analysis. As a witness, she finally found out what it meant to address her unbearable experience frontally and in public manner.

This chapter will follow the writing of Kofman[3] until she decided to dispense with "oblique" writing; until the moment when, following the death of her analyst, Kofman could no longer rely on an "ambassador of the wound"; the moment when she had to face trauma alone and chose to face it in writing. Ironically, Kofman's life answers Ferenczi's question about "more favourable circumstances". What her death exemplifies is the nature of "less favourable" or even "catastrophic circumstances".

I can only hope that her tragedy will contribute to the pragmatic, essay and error perspective on psychoanalysis that Ferenczi advocated in his *Diary* when he wrote, "Ideas are always tied to the vicissitudes in the patients' therapy. It is for therapy to determine either their validation or their dismissal" (Ferenczi, 1929, p. 419).

Sarah's story

Sarah Kofman's father, Rabbi Berek Kofman, was arrested on Thursday 16 July 1942 in the course of the "Vel' d'Hiv" round-up of Paris Jews (Kofman, 1986a). She had two mothers. In February, 1943, a raid by the Gestapo dispersed what was left of the family. Saved by the person who was to become her adopted mother—Mémé—Sarah disowned her birth mother. A father assassinated. A mother too many. Sarah Kofman took her own life half a century later, on Saturday 15 October 1994.

This is how the news of her death was reported:

> Sarah Kofman, born in Paris in 1933, was Professor of Philosophy at the University of Paris I – Sorbonne. She published 27 works, mostly with the publisher Galilée, all of them in the domain of philosophy ... In 1970, ... her first work, ... *The Childhood of Art* (Kofman 1988) presented a study of Freud's relation to art which earned her the recognition of Jacques Derrida ... In 1972, she ... published ... *Nietzsche and metaphor*. Sarah Kofman pursued her philosophical career on these two fronts, Freudian and Nietzschean. But, since the publication of *Rue Ordener, Rue Labat* (1996), Sarah Kofman had been going through a period of profound depression ... she had the feeling that she had put a full stop to her work by going back over her childhood ... (Ragon, 1994)

In its brevity, in its involuntary brutality, the journalist's account suggests a causal relationship between an act of self-expression and a death. It is suggested that, after years full of fruitful productivity, the creation of an autobiographical narrative caused a serious depression leading to suicide. Of course, the causal sequence could be inverted (depression triggering the autobiographical project) or even contested: throughout the thirty years or so during which Sarah Kofman never stopped writing, she had often spoken of her personal experiences and she had spoken of them in many different ways.

Sarah Kofman on her gravestone (photograph by Rachel Rosenblum).

We should, nevertheless, be aware that if she did indeed speak about these personal experiences, she also managed to avoid or exclude certain ways of doing so: accounts that were too direct. There are, however, styles of which she did readily avail herself. These styles are those that are, to use a vocabulary which she shares with Jacques Derrida, "pharmaceutic". They have the virtue of—this is a sort of *leit-motif* of Kofman's—"rendering the unbearable bearable".

Kofman's "pharmaceutic" styles are three in number. First and foremost, there are the works of exegesis, of philosophical reflection (Freud, Nietzsche, Plato, Derrida). Second, there are works in aesthetics: Sarah Kofman frequently analysed figurative works in which anguish is expressed (Goya), overcome (Rembrandt), or in which it undergoes metamorphosis (Leonardo da Vinci). Today, such works on figuration could be revisited as confessions. In a third style, Sarah Kofman devoted herself to intellectual autobiographies (Hoffmann, Wilde, and again Nietzsche). A strategy of *mise en abîme* allowed her to express herself through "heterobiography", to write (as Françoise Collin puts it) "in the textual body of the other". She managed in this way to narrate herself in the third person, to describe herself indirectly, to designate a series of "ambassadors" of herself, to avoid the perils of "subjectivation".

There remains a last style, which has nothing "pharmaceutic" about it: a direct and brutal style, with no possibility of displacement. It is made up of autobiographical fragments, of isolated events, of accounts of dreams. For a long time, this fourth style emerged only in the gaps between the other styles. Sarah Kofman's work ranged from one pharmaceutic style to another, in an attempt to avoid or to delay the intrusion of this fourth type of writing. But, one day, these styles tumbled into each other, came together. At some point, Sarah Kofman assembled the autobiographical fragments that had here and there broken the surface of her writings, and made out of them an explicit and continuous narrative. Neither fragmentary nor dreamlike, it is a testimony controlled by an "I", a confession from which all inessential elements have been banished so as to leave nothing but the brutal unity of tragedy. Death of the father. Conflict between the mothers. Horror linked to the exhibition of hatred.

The process which led to this convergence of styles and to the decision to write autobiographically took around thirty years. It is possible follow, from one style to the next, the narrative of the self that Sarah Kofman presents us with. Let us retrace the steps in an itinerary that veers between the "expressions" which kill and those which bring relief, between those which delay the conclusion and those which precipitate it, between those which prove irreversible and those which allow one to gain time. These steps are four in number.

1963–1976: The Childhood of Art *and its after-effects*

The Childhood of Art is a reflection on Freud, on figuration, and on the strategies (displacement, sublimation) which aim to "render bearable the unbearable". The cover of the book shows Leonardo da Vinci's famous "London cartoon". In it, Saint Mary and Saint Anne are holding two children who are playing (the baby Jesus and Saint John the Baptist). For Freud, whose analysis Sarah Kofman takes up here, the gentle smile that plays on the lips of Saint Anne is the sign of a lie without which the situation evoked would have been unbearable to the painter. Freud writes,

> Leonardo's childhood was remarkable in precisely the same way as this picture. He had had two mothers: first his true mother, Caterina, from whom he was torn away when he was between three and five, and then a young and tender step-mother, his father's wife . . .

According to Freud, as we know, the older woman in da Vinci's picture (Saint Anne) in fact corresponds to the mother whom Leonardo was taken from and, still according to Freud,

> the artist seems to have used the blissful smile of Saint Anne to disavow and to cloak the envy which the unfortunate woman (Caterina) felt when she was forced to give up her son to her better-born rival, as she had once given up his father as well.

"The mother's smile never existed", writes Sarah Kofman. In other words, the "blissful smile of Saint Anne is the result of a lie: it is the artist's disavowal of the suffering of his mother, and it masks the jealousy which she felt when she was forced to hand over her son to her rival".

When reading this text, it is hard not to think of the way in which Kofman came to love her adopted mother and disown her biological mother; of how she let the "mother" of rue Labat supplant in her heart the (real) mother of rue Ordener.

Sarah Kofman does not condemn Leonardo's lie: for her, the smile on the lips of Saint Anne is necessary, since it allows her to survive. Kofman sees this smile as the opposite of the violent feelings which take hold of her in the instant when she publicly accuses her mother;

the anguish she experiences when she perceives the shifting images of Miss Froy in Hitchcock's film *The Lady Vanishes*:

> the nice little old lady, Miss Froy, seated in the train opposite the sleeping heroine, vanishes . . . She is replaced by another woman who passes herself off as the first . . . The part that is always unbearable for me is to perceive, all of a sudden . . . the face of her replacement (who is wearing the clothes of the good lady . . .), a horribly hard, shifty face . . . menacing and false. (Kofman, 1996, p. 76)

The shift from the true Miss Froy to her impersonator feels like a sarcastic remake of the da Vinci picture. No beatific smiles; the harshness of truth.

1976–1983: the empty narrative and the full narrative, the adopted narrative and the orphaned narrative

During the period stretching from 1976 to 1983, Sarah Kofman looked for a form of expression that might convey truth without being deadly. From 1976 onwards, she raised most of the questions under discussion here. Can certain experiences actually be expressed? Can one express them without falsifying them? And, once uttered, can one find someone who wants or knows how to listen to them? What forms of reception should be provided for such expressions?

At the same time, she was writing texts that were only indirectly perilous. Here is the text of a dream. A very short fragment, very enigmatic: "On a book cover, 'I' read KAFKA . . . translated by Sa . . . Ko (a) f . . .". Sarah Kofman's commentary resembles certain remarks by Primo Levi.

> Why had "I" transformed myself into a translator of Kafka? Why had "I" changed my surname and forename in this way? What secret kinship could possibly link me to this person whose name I immediately associated with a trial, with guilt?

She sketches her own reply. The dream evokes "the punishment of the woman who aspired to deny her blood, efface her lowly origins, carry her head high" (Kofman, 1986a). Again, retrospectively, light can be thrown on Sarah Kofman's response: "denying one's blood" is rejecting one's mother. As with Primo Levi, Kafka turns here into an ambassador of lost feelings, of silenced emotions. He re-opens the paths of guilt. For Sarah Kofman, such a return of guilt, the resurgence of the repressed, the emergence of physical distress, become criteria for true expression. In a pivotal text, she contrasts this full expression to formal testimonies which might well be factual, but remain empty:

> I always wanted to recount my life . . . The whole beginning of my analysis was a long narrative . . . a continuous linear narrative. At no point did I lose the thread. I strung it together, knowing in advance what I was going to say. Not the slightest break, not the slightest hole, not the slightest fault-line where some lapsus might at last slip in, where something might slip through. Consequently, nothing happened. On the other side of the couch: nothing. "My life" was met with indifference. "Everything started" when "I" had nothing more to say, when "I" no longer knew where to start or where to finish. What I had narrated previously came back then but quite differently, discontinuously . . . or else never came back. . . . My mouth stopped being the place from which a reassuring discourse came forth—bocca della verita—and became a cavern spurting screams. (Kofman, 1986a, p. 79)

The Apollonian "Bocca della verita" is unworthy of trust. One must open up the "cavern spurting screams". But under what conditions? Sarah Kofman suggests that it is on condition that these cries do not just ring out in the void; on condition that a certain type of listening can receive, indeed embrace, the words that are spoken:

> The analyst's silence is unbearable. It not only means indifference to the events of my life, but conveys a devaluation of what is most private for me. Refusal of my gifts, of what comes forth from my womb, of what I produce: so my goods are just shit? In which case, better not give anything, not say anything; at least silence is golden. But I also find my own silence unbearable. Whence the imperious necessity of hearing my words taken up again and again. (Kofman, 1986a, p. 79)

As with Primo Levi, Kofman expresses her resentment for an unbearable silence, her need of a response, her feeling that such a response is lacking.

1983: a pivotal book. The fusion of styles

Ten years before her death, Sarah Kofman published a highly significant text: *Comment s'en sortir?* (1986b). The guarded optimism of the title (How to get out of it?) is belied by the very presentation of the work: grey and black cover displaying a chained giant. This bleak prisoner comes from Goya's black period. The anguish it elicits recurs in the middle of the book, through another illustration, also taken from Goya's black period: a faceless warlock faces two petrified individuals.

Starting with Goya's blind monsters, Kofman's reflections move across styles as she begins to work on autobiographical narrative and conceptual analysis at the same time. The autobiographical narrative follows a long reflection (stylistic and linguistic) on one of the medieval ways of expressing misfortune, "mala hora" (Cerquiglini, 1981). It discusses the syllable "*Mar*", a form that expresses at once hatred and anguish. For Sarah Kofman, it evokes at once the rue *Mar*-cadet and the following night*mare* [*cauche*-mar]:

> I am in a bedroom I remember from my childhood with my mother, my brothers and my sisters, at night. A bird comes in, a sort of bat with a human head crying out: *Woe* [*Malheur*] to you. *Woe* to you! Terrorised, my mother and I flee. We are in tears in the rue Marcadet. We know we are in very great danger and fear for our lives.

At this point, the narrative ceases to be that of a nightmare and becomes that of a fearsome childhood event.

> In February, 1943, almost 40 years ago, . . . at 8 in the evening (the "mala hora"), a man from the Kommandantur – the bird of ill omen – came to tell us, my mother and I (we were eating a vegetable soup in the kitchen) to hide away as quickly as possible, because we were on the list for that night . . . my father having already been rounded up on July 16 1942. My mother and I fled as fast as we could . . . We lived in rue Ordener so, in order to go to rue Labat where a woman generously sheltered us on the nights of raids, we took the endless rue Marcadet. On that forced nocturnal march, all the way along, I was petrified with anguish and vomited up my meal. The rest of the war we lived in hiding, rue Labat. (Kofman, 1986b, p. 18)

Horror takes the form of a flight by night. It is equated with the street (Marcadet) where the frightened child keeps on vomiting.

But the conceptual part of the book is also about horror and flight, particularly in the analysis devoted to the concept of "aporia" in Plato:

> Can one get out of what Plato calls an *aporia*? Can one get out of that impossible, nightmarish situation where one is suddenly disorientated, as though fallen into the depths of a well, helpless? . . . Can one get out of an infernal situation? Can one find a *poros*, that is to say, invent a stratagem in order to put an end to distress, trace a *path* leading from darkness to light? (Kofman, 1986b, p. 16)

It is I who emphasis the word *path*. For Sarah Kofman, it is indeed a question of a *path*. To find the *poros* is to "trace a path", to "invent a stratagem to put an end to distress". Finding the *poros* means bringing about "the opening of a passage across a chaotic stretch which it (the *poros*) transforms into a qualified, ordered space". Not finding the *poros* means remaining a prisoner of the chaos. The "aporia" thus merges with the "maritime abyss": it is the "sea widowed of routes", as Détienne and Vernant magnificently put it. At this point in the work of Kofman, conceptual analysis and autobiographical narrative seem to blend indissociably. Escaping from the aporia means coming out of the nightmare. Finding the "path" means escaping from the "maritime abyss", the "sea widowed of routes". Perhaps it also means escaping guilt. It means finding a street that one can follow without vomiting, a street which is not rue Marcadet.

This association between the *poros* and the street might seem arbitrary. But *Comment s'en sortir?* seems to be written with a view to producing such an association, constructed so as to enable the uncertain progression of autobiography towards the surface of the text. On the one hand, the chaos of the maritime abyss, the wordplay of the "sea widowed of routes"; on the other hand, what remains of the order preceding the catastrophe: the father's pen, an incitement to find the path . . . "Of him all I have left is the fountain pen . . . it is right in front of me on my desk and makes me write, write . . ." (Kofman, 1996, p. 3). Write? Why? "In order to solve precisely the question of the path, the *poros*, the way out. My numerous books were perhaps *byways* which I had to take in order to narrate 'that' . . .", Kofman concluded.

1984–1994: the transition to the first person

When, in 1994, Sarah Kofman decided to write her autobiography, she knew exactly what to expect. She had summarised the difficulties awaiting her in a work dating from 1987 (*Paroles suffoquées* (Stifled words)). She effectively found herself in the position of *having to* speak without *being able* to speak or be heard. She also knew that she would have to make sure that "language, too powerful, sovereign, did not come and take control of a completely aporetic situation, of total helplessness, of distress itself". She then wrote the unbearable text for which the rest of her works had been a continuous preparation. *Rue Ordener, rue Labat* was the raw exposure of the distress of a little girl torn between two mothers while her father was lost, rounded up, deported, and assassinated at Auschwitz:

> We find ourselves in the street, all six of us, pressed close together, sobbing very hard and wailing. When I first encountered in a Greek tragedy the well-known lament "*ô popoï, popoï, popoï*", I couldn't keep myself from thinking of that scene from my childhood where six children, their father gone, could only sob breathlessly, knowing they would never see him again, "oh papa, papa, papa". (Kofman, 1996, p. 7)

Sarah and her mother were saved by a woman from the neighbourhood.

> The lady from rue Labat was in full mourning. She was dressed in black, and I was struck by her blond hair and the soft melancholy in her blue eyes. ... The "lady" from rue Labat agreed to keep us "until we could find a solution" ... This lodging on rue Labat was to have been temporary. It lasted throughout the whole war. (pp. 35–36).

Sarah began loving this adopted mother, whom she called "Mémé". At the end of the war, she nevertheless had to return to her biological mother again. "Overnight I had to take leave of the woman I now loved more than my own mother. I had to share my mother's bed in a miserable hotel room on the Rue des Saules". Sarah disowned her mother so as not to have to leave Mémé.

The rest of her life was spent transposing or transfiguring the narrative of this repudiation, confessing her own hateful behaviour, so humiliating in its triviality:

> I was outraged to hear . . . my mother . . . falsely accuse the woman to whom we owed our lives and whom I loved so much. I in turn accused my mother, showing the court my thighs covered with bruises . . . The Jewish friend who had taken us in . . . confirmed that my mother beat me with a strap. (Kofman, 1996 p. 60)

This was an episode for which Kofman would never forgive herself. The woman upon whom Sarah heaped reproaches was not only her mother, but also a victim. Having brought evidence against her mother, she would also testify against herself. In the last pages of the book she intimates that she did also betray "Mémé".

> . . . Mémé died recently, in a hospice. . . . Seriously disabled, half blind, she couldn't do anything anymore except listen to 'great music' . . . I was unable to attend her funeral. But I know that at her grave the priest recalled how she had saved a little Jewish girl during the war. (Kofman, 1996, p. 84)

Posthumous texts: a lesson in sublimation

Written at the end of her life and published after her death, Sarah Kofman's last two works are equivocal testaments. Both address the question of the unseen or the unsaid. Her study of Oscar Wilde's *Portrait of Dorian Gray* (*L'imposture de la beauté*, 1995a) could be applied to her own texts.

> The portrait's first transformation is the one brought about by the writing which displays the painting only in words. While these words expose the painting they also conceal it from sight, thus rendering the unbearable and monstrous metamorphosis bearable.

One would have to change very little here to define a Kofmanian "poetics". Render the unbearable bearable. Speak out the "ghastly" tale, but as if it were someone else's tale, the motive of other people's images. Make sure that the very gesture that exposes also conceals from sight. It is this same gesture (expose, conceal from sight) that Sarah Kofman points to at the heart of one of the most powerful of Rembrandt's canvases, *Dr Tulp's Anatomy Lesson* (1632). At the centre of the picture, a table and a bloodless corpse, partly dissected. Surrounding the table, doctors in dark clothes. Apart from one exception, nobody pays attention to the body of the exhibited dead person. No horror. No compassion. Everyone is listening to the explanations of Doctor Tulp, who points to a vast open book at the foot of the corpse. "The lesson to be drawn from this anatomy lesson is not . . . that of a *memento mori*", writes Sarah Kofman. "It is not a triumph of death, but a triumph over death; and this, not through the life of illusion, but through that of the *speculative*". In order to conceal horror, a new strategy is brought up here.

> If the spectator of the anatomy lesson is not gripped by anguish at the sight of this painting, and can even gaze at it in complete serenity, it is because he is dealing with an image, a representation which has a pharmaceutic function.

In fact, the aspiring doctors have in front of them

> not a subject but an object, a pure technical instrument which one of them manipulates so as to have a hold on the truth of life . . . The dead man (and the opening up of his body) are seen solely as producing an opening onto life to which they appear to hold the key. Fascination is displaced, and with this displacement, anguish is repressed, the unbearable rendered bearable. (Kofman, 1995b, p. 43)

The violence enacted on a corpse transformed into an instrument of knowledge and culture is, thus, referred back to the founding act of the corporate body of doctors. Death is "warded off". Like the stratagems employed by Oscar Wilde, Rembrandt's "demonstration" rejoins Kofman's procedures. One dissolves horror by attempting to think it; by moving from the wide-open corpse to the whiteness of the page; by seeing not chaos but the quest for a *poros*.

As Derrida emphasises (1997), Sarah Kofman's commentary is far from being simply descriptive. It asserts the value of a certain form of repression. Instead of rejecting it as mere negativity (negation, denegation, lie, concealment, dissimulation), Sarah Kofman senses in this repression . . . "a cunning affirmation of life, the impossible need for survival". Ironically, Kofman's advocacy of survival reaches us in a posthumous text.

In more favourable circumstances?

Guilt, shame, and the phantasised public

As Sarah Kofman's experience shows, testimony is not merely a question of sharing information or of reconstructing facts (as in history), but of making those facts public *in the first person*. In the testimonies concerned here, the point is not merely one of bearing witness ("I saw"), but one of bearing witness about what one did ("I was present and this is what I did "). Sarah Kofman preferred her adopted mother, free and cheerful, to her biological mother, demanding and hounded. Going through similar feelings of guilt, Primo Levi cries out, citing Dante, "[I] haven't usurped anyone's bread". He did not, indeed, eat anyone else's bread, but he did not always share the bread he had. Or he did share it, with some, but not with others (Levi, 1988). He obviously could not share it with the thousands of beings who needed it. There remains the guilt linked to the fact that he sometimes refused to give it, or had "chosen" those he would give some to. Every survivor, at some time or another, has made one of those terrible choices. Should the survivor keep silent?

Either one keeps the tragedy for oneself, and, as Primo Levi says, one "is burnt" by it (in Sarah Kofman's words, one becomes its "sarcophagus"). Or else one discloses it, but this disclosure does not necessarily efface it. It publicises it, makes it official, removes it from other people's ignorance. A shameful knowledge is thus shared, but with a paradoxical result. As Kofman puts it, the narrative of the survivors exposes them doubly. It resurrects their guilt with respect to the victims; it also exposes them to the judgement of those who learn what they did. No matter how sympathetic, these readers are always potential judges and, sometimes, effective censors. Sarah Kofman's confession was published. It was addressed to a public. This is far from being an incidental detail. Who is, indeed, the public for such witnesses? What sort of transference does it trigger? Is it a companion or a judge? In the writings of Primo Levi, for example, the public is present, but as a disquieting entity, one that is either indifferent or hostile. There are those who do not pay attention, who ignore your plight. There are also those who pay negative attention. The witness finds himself absorbed by the monstrosity of what he recounts. He becomes "sacred", feels put at a distance. These are horribly unfavourable circumstances. Can there be better ones?

The "good" interlocutor

"More favourable circumstances" are largely concerned with the persona of the victim's interlocutor. The discourse of guilt calls for an interlocutor who is not only capable of receiving the narrative, but also of resituating it in its full context; of providing what Laub calls "the compass of history". The discourse of shame presupposes an interlocutor with whom the shameful situation can be replayed, someone to help you regain composure; someone in the face of whom one can re-establish a semblance of dignity. But does such a "good interlocutor" exist?

In the case of massive trauma, the ideal interlocutor is entrusted with a task worthy of Orpheus. This task consists in finding the *poros*, the path that allows the speaker–victim to be led back among the living. This task is difficult, almost impossible. Perhaps the figure of the good interlocutor has yet to be invented. Yet, I believe many of its features can be delineated.

In positive terms, let me first stress that such an interlocutor must be an actual person, not a "persona ficta", not a public. Sarah Kofman's plight shows that psychoanalysts ought to avoid any behaviour that would even distantly resemble collective indifference. Their listening should literally "receive" the survivor's words, grant them hospitality, instead of letting them sink into silence, a point that was made by Ferenczi himself when he wrote, "The presence of someone with whom one can share and communicate . . . can heal the trauma. Personality is re-assembled, 'healed' (like glue)" (Ferenczi, 1932, p. 201).

Another requirement inspired by Ferenczi to be met by the ideal interlocutor consists in responding to the doubts entertained by trauma victims as to the very reality of their own experiences. As noted by the Hungarian analyst, these are experiences which they might remember, but often do not believe in. Perhaps these traumatic events never really took place? Perhaps did they merely occur as psychic events? The ideal interlocutor, in this case, needs to be an authenticating witness. His task is one of validating the reality of the trauma. As Laub puts it, the "listener–witness" is responsible for establishing that "the victim is not the perpetrator and that . . . the historical event, indeed, took place" (Laub, personal communication, 2006). This importance of the authenticating witness has also been highlighted by Gubrich-Simitis (2010), in a paper significantly entitled: "Reality testing in place of interpretation" (p. 11).

To further delineate the characteristics of a good interlocutor, I would like to refer to the work of psychoanalyst Sidney Stewart. Stewart explicitly transgressed established psychoanalytic protocols in order to enter the sort of conversation needed by his traumatised patients (1991). His performance exemplifies, in many ways, what an "ideal" interlocutor should do. Stewart accompanied his patients; he shared with them his own traumatic experiences.[4]

To use Laub's phrase, Stewart entered "the eye of the hurricane". In a way, Stewart acted in Ferenczian style: "It is by revealing his own feelings of anxiety and guilt – Ferenczi writes in *The Clinical Diary* that the psychoanalyst allows the patient to reveal feelings of a like nature" (Stewart,1991, referring to Ferenczi, 1932, p. 257).

Kofman's story in Ferenczi's words

The ideal interlocutor can also be defined through negative traits. The fear of being on her own transpires in Kofman's writing when she laments the coldness of classical analysis, the despair of not being accompanied, the remoteness of her analyst. Yet, even though the silence of her analyst was unbearable, the analyst was there. Things changed radically when he died. Kofman found herself with no one to "take up her words", and this ended in tragedy. Kofman's tragedy is already accounted for almost sixty years earlier in the writings of Ferenczi.

Ferenczi points to the existence of two degrees of avoidance in response to a major trauma. The first is anaesthetic. It consists in the avoidance of feeling or emotion. The second is perceptual. It consists in an absence of perception. "Against an impression that is not perceived, it is impossible to defend oneself". But, even if (as in the case of Kofman) there is no radical avoidance, no erasure of the trauma, a significant transformation occurs. In response to a first trauma, the trauma victim splits in the two complementary roles of "victim" and "guardian angel". But imagine that a second traumatisation occurs. This "re-traumatisation" reveals the powerlessness of the guardian. The victim feels utterly unprotected. This, Ferenczi writes, might lead to tragic consequences: but if a new and stronger traumatism occurs, the "guardian angel" is proved impotent; thus, unless something favourable happens at the last minute in the real world, committing suicide looks like the only option left (Ferenczi, 1934).

This "something favourable", which may counterbalance the suicidal impulse, consists for the patient in not being alone when facing the new traumatic struggle. We cannot offer patients the help they needed as children. Yet, the very fact of offering help now gives them an impulsion for a new life, closes the chapter of irreversible losses, represents a first step towards accepting what life still has to offer, instead of rejecting it all at once (Ferenczi, 1934).

This something favourable turned out not to be available to Sarah Kofman, whose "heterobiographies" consisted in conjuring a number of "guardian angels", of "ambassadors of the wound", of friendly figures that allowed her for many years to interpose culture between herself and her trauma. But three crucial events happened. Kofman discovered she had cancer. She started writing in the first person. Her psychoanalyst, Serge Viderman, died. In other words, Kofman found herself facing on her own the double traumatisation of cancer and speaking out her past. By writing a frontal, often brutal autobiography, Kofman had dismissed her cultural "guardian angels". Had Serge Viderman been able to offer the sort of help that Ferenczi speaks about, had he been capable of closing " the chapter of irreversible losses", he was no longer there to do so. Suicide could then be felt like a logical outcome of Kofman's situation.

Ironically, of course, Ferenczi's scenario also applies to himself. While Ferenczi looked forward to his own trauma being repeated in "more favourable circumstances", Freud turned down the role which his disciple expected of him; a role which meant confirming the reality of Ferenczi 's experience. Submitted to a chain of retraumatisations, Ferenczi had to face his plight on his own. In his case, as in Kofman's (albeit for different reasons), no one was there to be entrusted with the narrative of the painful experience; no one was there to take it up, to confirm it or share it. Both seem to have died of never being treated to the luxury of "more favourable circumstances".

Ferenczi's own tragedy

Let us conclude this paper by briefly retracing the last moments of Ferenczi's life with a special focus on the "tragic encounter between Freud and Ferenczi".

In the early 1930s, the long friendship between Freud and Ferenczi gives way to an open disagreement concerning "the relative weight of internal and external reality" (Bergmann, 1996, p. 145). Ferenczi pleads with Freud, trying to convince him to accept the changes he is introducing. He has valid reasons to plead with Freud, since his "real-istic" approach to traumatism (the acknowledgement that a trauma-tism could be caused by an actual event) does not, in his perspective, preclude the existence of a phantasmatic dimension. Yet, for Freud himself, eventually followed by the guardians of a strict Freudian orthodoxy, the possibility of a traumatic occurrence that would be based on an actual event feels like a regression towards earlier, pre-psychoanalytic theories. Freud maintains his refusal to accept the validity of Ferenczi's account of trauma and tries dissuading him from publicly reading the paper Ferenczi prepared for the 1932 Wiesbaden conference, a paper whose famous thesis on "The confusion of tongues" has since become a classic. When Ferenczi persists and reads the paper anyway, Freud tries to prevent the essay from being published in the *Internationale Zeitschrift für Psychoanalyse*, a move that will initiate a long tradition of ostracism. (Reactivated by Ernest Jones, a holy alliance against the Hungarian analyst is still in place, more than twenty years after his death. Not only is Ferenczi's sticking to his positions still seen as a challenge to the psychoanalytic movement, but his writings are dismissed as manifestations of a pathological disor-der.) The inquisitorial nature of this "excommunication" process is forcefully analysed by Bonomi (1999), and also by Dupont (1995), Martin Bergmann (1996).

Yet, the tension between Freud and his disciple is more than theo-retical. We know that Ferenczi's trauma theory is largely inferred from his own experience. Guillaumin reminds us that Ferenczi's observation of "a dream by a patient" is in fact an observation about Ferenczi himself. Guillaumin also notes that Ferenczi was "dominated by the fear of a real identification with the aggressors of his childhood, and that of submitting his patients to similar traumas" (Guillaumin, 1995, p. 113). Ferenczi feels that his brief analysis with Freud, some fifteen years earlier, has never properly addressed his childhood trauma. In a veiled accusation, Ferenczi attributes the onset of the illness from which he eventually dies on May 22, 1933, to his former analyst's shortcomings.

> In my case a blood crisis arose when I realised that not only can I not rely on the protection of the "higher power" but on the contrary, I shall be trampled under foot by this indifferent power as soon as I go my own way and not his. (Ferenczi, 1932, p. 257)

Combining the theoretical and the personal, the public and the private, failure and disawoval, Freud's rejection proves overwhelming to Ferenczi, who finds himself in the nightmarish position which Primo Levi will poignantly express, decades later. Ferenczi's plight almost literally exemplifies the dream in which the Italian writer sees himself talking to a group of people, each of which silently stands up and leaves. Ferenczi's presence is discomforting. Like Coleridge's ancient mariner, he keeps telling a story no one wants to hear. He is the messenger of bad news, the reminder of a reality that goes against both theoretical blindness and historical denial. When he suggests that the progress of Nazism might represent a threat for European Jews and that it might be time for Freud to leave Austria, Freud ironically dismisses the suggestion, which his letters further deprecate as delusional. The problem, of course, was not with Ferenczi's "delusions", but with Freud's amazing denial of reality. But this we know with hindsight. Bonomi put it beautifully, when he wrote that Freud chose not to hear: he elected to take "flight into sanity" (Bonomi, 1999).

Ferenczi 's position was doomed. What could he do when his theoretical opponent was not only his friend and mentor but also his model and former analyst? Could he enter a controversy whose judge was also the other party? Dupont stresses the "desperate" dimension of Ferenczi's "quest to obtain Freud's support in his perilous exploration" (Dupont, 1995).

Ferenczi was not only a loyal, respectful opponent. He was, and felt, a victim. He was and felt "wronged". In Lyotard's words (1983), Ferenczi's disagreement with Freud was much worse than a dispute. It was a *differend*.

A *differend* is that which comes about when "a conflict opposing two or more disputants is judged . . . in the idiom of one of the parties while the wrong suffered by the other is not signified in that idiom" (Lyotard, 1983, p. 9). Thus, the plaintiff of a *differend* emits a "grievance that cannot be heard". The *differend* emerges as a result of the plaintiff's deprivation of the means with which to prove or even express the wrong suffered (Lyotard, 1983, p. 9). "The plaintiff is divested of the means to argue and becomes for that reason a victim" (Lyotard, 1983, p. 9). Disagreements in which one of the parties enjoys the performative power of pronouncing factuality are doomed to turn into "*differends*". This is exactly what takes place between Ferenczi and the psychoanalytic institution. Situating the origin of a psychic trauma mainly in external reality triggers a long sequence of reactions from those (Freud's institutionally appointed heirs) who dogmatically exclude the very possibility of an external causation of such traumas. Not only is it important for them to deny (or underestimate) how much traumas can have a real origin, but saying so exposes Ferenczi to being stigmatised as "delusional" or "paranoid". Like other bearers of unwanted (theoretical, or, in earlier times, theological) news, Ferenczi is excommunicated, condemned to "social death". Indeed this "social death" and the enforced silence that turns a plaintiff into a victim did not end with Ferenczi's physical death. It is this death that I wish to discuss now.

To say that Ferenczi's personal trauma was not repeated in "more favourable circumstances" is an understatement. The trauma was declared inexistent. By being asked to repudiate the realist elements whose weight he had reintroduced in trauma theory, Ferenczi was also being asked to repudiate his own memories and his own construction of self. He was invited to see this construction as "false and untrustworthy". This gave the Hungarian analyst a choice of two possibilities.

The first was "amputating part of himself", rejecting his own diagnosis and accepting to attribute an intrapsychic origin to his trauma. But Ferenczi felt a bit too old for such an exercise. He was understandably reluctant at the idea of repudiating both his theoretical construct and his personal history.

The other possibility was death. Freud's rejection and "pernicious anaemia" occur almost at the same time. Yet, it is important to note that in Ferenczi's mind (and in his clinical diary), it is the rejection that in a way causes the onset of the illness. Ferenczi ponders his situation. "Is the choice here, one between dying and rearranging myself, and this at the age of fifty nine?" Here is his answer: ". . . a certain strength in my psychological makeup seems to persist, so that instead of falling ill psychologically, I can only destroy or be destroyed in my organic depths" (Ferenczi, 1933, p. 213). Ferenczi seems to opt for "organic destruction". He dies that very year at age fifty-nine.

Did Freud's rejection actually lead to illness? This, at least, is how the situation was perceived by Ferenczi. Freud had turned down the role that his disciple would have expected of him, a role which meant confirming the reality of his traumatic experience. Put together, Freud's unavailability and Ferenczi's retraumatisation added up to create the worst possible circumstances.

Acknowledgements

Some of the ideas presented here were discussed in the *Revue Française de Psychanalyse*. My thanks to the editors. My thanks also to my first translator, Saskia Brown, and to my first reader, Daniel Dayan, who acquainted me with Jean François Lyotard's concept of "Le différend". My thanks finally to my intellectual hosts for this project: Judit Szekacs and Tom Keve.

Notes

1. This article was written in response to Sarah Kofman's suicide. I had a personal relation to the philosopher, and when I read her book, *Rue Ordener, rue Labat* (1996), I wondered about the connection between her death and the memoir she had just published. I devoted many years to exploring this connection, starting with a close reading of Kofman's "Ma vie et la psychanalyse". My exploration did not happen in a void. While working on the subject, I realised that other authors had been involved in the same type of enquiry. There was, in fact, a huge volume of litera-ture on historical traumas and survivors' testimonies. This literature was remarkably discussed by Dayan-Rosenman (2007) and Waintrater (2003). I analysed myself over more than four years of psychoanalytic thinking in regard to Shoah (Rosenblum, 2012). Like other analysts of my genera-tion, I was treating victims of gigantic traumatisms, knew these trauma-tisms were historically attested, and tried to find new ways to address the

victims' plight. Yet, many established approaches seemed inadequate, counterproductive, or plainly dangerous. Such was Ernest Jones' dogmatic notion that psychoanalysis exists only in one form (the interpretation paradigm) and that the model of neurosis applies to all situations. Such was the fact of suppressing the weight of traumatic reality by treating trauma as pure phantasy: this amounted to reproducing in theoretical form the denial of those trauma victims who choose to sacrifice their mental integrity in order not to believe in the reality of certain unspeakable events and in the responsibility of their perpetrators. By contrast, Sandor Ferenczi's "realist" approach to trauma anticipated and acknowledged many of the problems we were encountering. This approach was characterised by pragmatism over concerns for "purity", by flexibility over dogma. One could account for both the real occurrence of a traumatism and for its phantasmatic dimension. Ferenczi proved that the interpretative approach, and the "accompaniment" approach could be complementary.

2. Some individuals are more "resilient" than others. It depends on who they where before the trauma occurred, on the seriousness of the trauma, on how early in life it occurred. Boris Cyrulnik's notion of "resilience" could help understanding why narrative can be lethal in the case of some trauma victims and the not in the case of others. Yet, in a recent book, Cyrulnik describes resilience not in terms of a quality of the person, but in terms of a work, labour, or strategy. Thus, he speaks of a "travail de résilience" (Cyrulnik, 2010). This "travail" involves distancing one's traumatic experience; describing it from the outside, as if it were that of a third party. Defining resilience in terms of a "strategy" amounts, of course, to what I have been proposing in numerous essays (Rosenblum, 1998, 2000, 2002, 2004, 2005) in which I discussed the role of "screen-texts" and *heterobiographies* (speaking of others as an indirect way of speaking about oneself). Significantly, Cyrulnik's last two books are personal and they often borrow the words of others. Among such others are Georges Perec, whose title, *Je me souviens* (Cyrulnik, 2003) is picked up by Cyrulnik. Similarly, the title of my essay "Peut on mourir de dire?" (Rosenblum, 2000) becomes that of Cyrulnik's *Mourir de dire* (2010). Appropriating phrases and sometimes concepts seems—among other things—to allow Cyrulnik to address personal issues with the type of distance I have been advocating.

3. For a complete bibliography of Sarah Kofman's works, see *Cahiers du Grif*, 3: 171–190. Paris: Descartes, 1997.

4. The choice by analysts of the 1970s of an extremely reserved attitude, an attitude meant to avoid the traps of suggestion, has been vastly criticised

(for instance by André Green) and especially in regard to borderline and traumatic cases. Sarah Kofman herself was an early and vocal critic of the strategy of "silence".

Contrasting with this strategy, here is a vignette illustrating the way in which a negative therapeutic reaction was creatively overcome by the transgressive wisdom of an analyst. This vignette illustrates the possibility of a "poros", of a positive outcome. The example at hand is that of Sidney Stewart's treatment of a patient he calls Dr Esther.

An established Jewish scientist consults Sidney Stewart (Stewart, 1991) for memory problems. In order not to forget, she lives with a notebook attached to her wrist. Sidney Stewart calls her Dr Esther. Noticing the number tattooed on her arm, he learns that she, her mother, and her sister were taken to the death camps when she was ten. Nazis had burst into her family's apartment on the fifth floor and thrown her father out of a window. She is now forty-five.

Dr Esther is ambivalent. She chooses Sidney Stewart because he has been an inmate of a concentration camp, but she wants him not to be Jewish. She wishes him to be close, but seeks a linguistic distance, using English to relate her traumatic experiences, while remaining relatively protected from their affective dimension.

Rapidly, the analysis comes to a standstill. Dr Esther experiences angry fits, keeps losing weight. Wondering whether he is on the wrong track, Stewart has a dream. This is the heart of winter in a concentration camp in Manchuria. A man is about to die and holds a rice bowl in his hand. His best friend crawls to where he lies and tries to steal the bowl of rice, forcing open the dying man's fingers. The dying man gazes at the thief. A witness to this scene, Stewart feels shame.

After much hesitation, feeling he is about to do something transgressive, Stewart tells Dr Esther his dream. The result is an explosion of memories that Dr Esther had, until then, succeeded in silencing. In earlier interviews, Dr Esther had merely said that her father had been thrown out of a window by the Nazis. She now goes on to tell the rest of her story. Young Esther is with her mother and her younger sister in a line of women walking toward the gas chambers. During a moment of inattention, she slips out of that line, thus escaping death. She will never see her mother or sister again. When she tells the story, Dr Esther starts sobbing.

This marks a turning point in the cure. Sidney Stewart can now move to the analysis of Esther's early childhood, address her feelings of envy when her mother became pregnant and her sister was born. (Clearly these archaic guilt feelings became imbricated with those of the survivor.)

Meanwhile, Dr Esther's fear of forgetting disappears. The scientist discovers that her memory functions normally.

This case seems to end quite well. Many factors can be held responsible for the happy ending. Some involve choices made by the patient (the use of a foreign language as a way of distancing affect); some involve choices of the analyst himself, and, first of all, that of breaking rules by "lending" the patient his own "Manchurian dream", one in which he appears, if not in the guise of a thief, at least in the role of a silent witness, of an accomplice, to an appalling action.

How do we explain such a success? Through the position he has chosen to adopt, that of the psychoanalyst as *Doppelgänger*, Sidney Stewart shoulders part of Esther's shame, makes it lighter. The psychoanalyst's shame enables Dr Esther to relate to her own.

References

Bergmannn, M. (1996). The tragic encounter between Freud and Ferenczi. In: *Ferenczi's Turn in Psychoanalysis* (pp. 145–159). New York: New York University Press.

Bonomi, C. (1999). Flight into sanity. Jones' allegation of Ferenczi's mental deterioration revisited. *International Journal of Psychoanalysis, 80*: 507–542.

Cerquiglini, B. (1981). *La parole médiévale*. Paris: Minuit.

Chasseguet-Smirgel, J. (2000). Trauma et croyance. *Revue Française de Psychanalyse, 64*: 39–46.

Cyrulnik, B. (2003). *Je me souviens Paris*. Paris: L'esprit du temps.

Cyrulnik, B. (2010). *Mourir de dire; la Honte*. Paris: Odile Jacob.

Dayan-Rosenman, A. (2007). *Les Alphabets de la Shoah*. Paris: CNRS.

Derrida, J. (1997). *Cahiers du Grif, 3*: 131. Paris: Descartes.

Dupont, J. (1995). Preface to Ferenczi, S (1932).

Ferenczi, S. (1929). Letter to Sigmund Freud. In: E. Falzeder & E. Brabant (Eds.), *The Correspondence of Sigmund Freud and Sándor Ferenczi Volume 3, 1920–1933*. Cambridge, MA: Harvard University Press, 2000.

Ferenczi, S. (1932). *Clinical Diary of Sándor Ferenczi*, J. Dupont (Ed.). Cambridge, MA: Harvard University Press, 1995.

Ferenczi, S. (1933). Confusion of tongues between adults and the child. In: *Final Contributions to the Problems and Methods of Psycho-Analysis* (pp. 156–167). London: Hogarth Press, 1955 [reprinted, London: Karnac, 1994].

Ferenczi, S. (1934). Gedanken über das Trauma. *Internationale Zeitschrift für Psychoanalyse*, XX: 12–15.

Gubrich-Simitis, I. (2010). Reality testing in place of interpretation. *Psychoanalytic Quarterly*, 1: 37–69.

Guillaumin, J. (1995). Ferenczi, La mort et l' auto-analyse. In: T. Bokanowski, K. Kelley-Lainé, & G. Pragier (Eds.), *Sándor Ferenczi* (pp. 113–124). Paris: RFP Monographs. PUF.

Kofman, S. (1986a). Tomb for a proper name, F. Bartkowski (Trans.), Autobiographical writings in *Substance*, 49, 1986, original version: Ma vie et la psychanalyse, *Première livraison*, 4, reprinted in *Cahiers du GRIF*, Paris: Descartes, 1997.

Kofman, S. (1986b). *Comment s'en sortir?* Paris, Galilée. Partly translated into English as Nightmare, *Substance*, 49, Autobiographical writings, 1986, and as Beyond Aporia, D. Macey (Trans.). *Warwick Studies in Philosophy and Literature*, 7–44, 1988.

Kofman, S. (1987). *Paroles suffoquées*. Paris: Galilée.

Kofman, S. (1988). *The Childhood of Art: An Interpretation of Freud's Aesthetic*, W. Woodhill (Trans.). New York: Columbia University Press.

Kofman, S. (1995a). *L'imposture de la beauté*. Paris: Galilée.

Kofman, S. (1995b). La mort conjuguée (*Dr Tulp's Anatomy Lesson*, 1632). *La part de l'œil*, 11: 41–46.

Kofman, S. (1996). *Rue Ordener, rue Labat*, A. Smock (Trans.). Lincoln, NB: University of Nebraska Press.

Laub, D. (1992a). Bearing witness, or the vicissitudes of listening. In: S. Felman & D. Laub, *Testimony: Crises of Witnessing in Literature, Psychoanalysis, and History* (pp. 57–74). New York: Routledge.

Laub, D. (1992b). An event without a witness: truth, testimony and survival. In: S. Felman & D. Laub, *Testimony: Crises of Witnessing in Literature, Psychoanalysis, and History* (pp. 75–92). New York: Routledge.

Levi, P. (1988). *Collected Poems*, R. Feldman & B. Swann (Trans.). London: Faber and Faber, also available at: www.poemhunter.com/poem/the-survivor.

Lyotard, J. F. (1983). *Le Différend*. Paris: Minuit.

Ragon, M. (1994). Nécrologie de Sarah Kofman. *Libération*, 18 Otober 1994.

Rosenblum, R. (1998). Mourir de dire. *Bulletin de la Société Psychanalytique de Paris*, 50: 15–19.

Rosenblum, R. (2000). Peut-on mourir de dire? Sarah Kofman, Primo Lévi. *Revue Française Psychanalyse*, 64: 113–137.

Rosenblum, R. (2002). And till the ghastly tale is told: Primo Levi, Sarah Kofman. *European Judaism*, Berghahn Books, New York

Rosenblum, R. (2004). Childhood lost and found: Benjamin Wilkomirski, living out and screen formations. In: J. Szekacs-Weisz & I. Ward (Eds.), *Lost Childhood* (pp. 193–206). London: Imago.

Rosenblum, R. (2005). Cure ou répétition du trauma. *Revue Française de Psycho-somatique, 28*: 69–90

Rosenblum, R. (2009). Postponing trauma: the dangers of telling. *International Journal of Psychoanalysis, 90*: 1319–1340.

Rosenblum, R. (2012).Trauma and psychoanalysis. *IPA Newsletter*. In press.

Semprun, J. (1994).). *L'écriture ou la vie*. Paris: Gallimard [*Literature or Life*, L. Coverdale (Trans.). New York: Viking, 1998].

Stewart, S. (1991). *Revue Française de Psychanalyse*, "Dr Esther" in "*Mémoires de l'Inhumain. Du trauma à la créativité*. Paris: Campagne Première, 2004. First published in vol. 55, pp. 957–975, also in "Dr Esther" in "*Mémoires de l'Inhumain. Du trauma à la créativité*. Paris: Campagne Première, 2004.

Waintrater, R. (2003). *Sortir du genocide*. Paris: Payot.

PART V
CLOSE TO THE BODY

CHAPTER TWELVE

Psychosomatics and technique

Jonathan Sklar

The writer Aharon Appelfeld, when eight years old, witnessed the pogrom in his home town of Czernowitz. He saw the murder of his mother and, separated from the rest of his family, survived by scavenging in the forests. Remembrance was complicated, he thought, by his having been too young a child to process much of what he saw. The past remains entirely physical for him: "etched inside my body but not in my memory". After more than half a century, his feet still cause tension in his legs and this instantly transfers him back to the years in hiding. The very act of sitting or standing can conjure up hellish visions of packed railway stations. Rotting straw or the call of a bird trigger visceral memories deep within his body (*The Observer Book Review*, 21 August 2005).

The ability to free associate is both protected and inhibited by the movement of affect into the body acting as a container and away from the mind with thoughts and associative strands. A particular part of the body with its physicality, such as a feeling of body rigidity or a

A version of this paper has appeared in *Landscapes of the Dark*, by Jonathan Sklar, London: Karnac, 2011.

certain sequence of movements, can contain that which must not be felt and integrated.

Appelfeld conveys material that is extreme and alarming. At some time he saw, heard, and felt leaving the victim in a state of uncompre-hending terror, responding, perhaps, by immobility, being struck dumb, and fleeing the scene to survive. This is descriptive of over-whelming trauma, even more for his being a child, who had not yet developed enough mental capacity—although what adult has! Yet, the mind needs protection from the impact of massive affect: a move from psyche to soma. The body takes over as the contours of associations, but away from a capacity to free associate. Thus, one finds a patient who adopts particular positions on the couch, such as a certain rigidity of limbs, or never moving, as a means of concealing earlier trauma, far distant from some terrible knowing. Of course, there might be free associations, but only up to a point, after which one can notice the inhi-bition in the body. This acts to both conceal and reveal. It is as well to notice such positional structures in order to make possible the move-ment away from being stuck and towards mental curiosity. Putting it into words moves psychic energy from thing (body) presentation to word presentation that enables affect to move from an attachment to the body to that of the clinical dyad. This requires, as with the rest of an analysis, time to work through the new-found memories in terms of past relationships. The patient, in his psychosomatic "stuckness", is alone and does not expect, or wish for, the intervention of the other. The unconscious expectation is that the other is not there to help and often (invariably?) this has historical truth, since adults have not protected the infant from trauma and might even have caused it.

There is a new possibility in the telling: that the listener who is benign can hear the patient, invariably for the first time. Critically, the move from soma to psyche contains a new beginning. This, under the everyday surface noise of the analysand, might be an unexpected and new position. The patient might know that he or she is being listened to by the other for the first time.

A young woman, in analysis for several years at five times a week, had suffered the consequences of being abandoned by her parents as a teenager. They and the younger siblings all left for a new life abroad. Much understanding had been excavated over time about her early life, the abandonment in her adolescence, and its impact on her self and her relationships. In particular, there was evidence of a constant maternal paranoia always supported by the father. At times of either great stress in life, or when it was moving along quite smoothly, there would be a return to the physical symptom of retching. Usually, this would be when she was imagining a good evening, a lovely meal and becoming closer to her boyfriend, or, similarly, when she was on the point of attaining some achievement at work. Then the symptom would kick in, leaving her fearful that it would happen outside her imagination and leave her in need of a toilet to be alone in order to vomit. Subsequently, such a cycle would leave her body feeling relieved but she would feel terrible in her mind.

Clearly, someone or something was making the patient feel sick to such an extent that it needed to be got rid of. Here is some material from a session prior to the end of term.

> *Patient*: I wanted to say I didn't want to leave yesterday but I couldn't say it. You are right; I do try and keep my thoughts sterile. I have other thoughts and I cannot, must not, think them. I hate this. I wondered if your wife breast-fed. My mother hated the idea and didn't . . . She couldn't bear the mess. It has to be kept clean and sterile.

> *Therapist's interpretation*: As long as there are no free associations here in case they are dirty, you keep your mother content.

> *Patient*: It's true I know such associations are good for me. I will miss you. I hate you for being away and then I'm on my own. It is far more important that I want to know. I think of the interpretations that I make about the break but it seems sterile. I'm like my mother. I pick away at the argument.

> *Therapist's interpretation*: So the danger in the break is that you and your mother's arguments are putting our work and me down.

> *Patient*: When you are away I call you horrible things . . . Johnny.

> *Therapist's interpretation*: A contraceptive! (and also my name) . . .

> *Patient*: I knew you would say that.

> *Therapist's interpretation*: . . . and the use of it is to keep you sterile from analytic dirty thoughts.

> *Patient*: I have realised that also I have put the word "anal" as an abbreviation in my diary for sessions. Anyone would see it as anal. But yesterday I did feel better as talking beyond the sterile helped me. I was so relieved breaking through the barrier.

Concrete metaphors utilise a contraceptive cover to separate dirty words and dirty thoughts, imprison the patient, and keep her alone. It is a mental barrier to the free flow of unconscious and conscious mental life across the divide to the other. The mother is disdainful of intimacy and desires the utmost cleanliness. The symptom of retching is what the retch does as a means of messing up the purity. Vomiting is a symptom that attempts to break through the contraceptive barrier, although it is hard for the patient to acknowledge the metaphor as a need for a healthy messing up as a way of breaking through the sterility. It is likely that the symptom also contains the patient's unconscious idea that she was not wanted as a baby, as if she is enacting a pregnant mother vomiting her. Indeed, she has had thoughts that mother tried to abort her. So, the symptom of vomiting contains the idea of a woman pregnant and rejecting.

Since that piece of work, the patient has been able to be much more successful in her professional life and has begun living with her boyfriend. The symptom has not been in evidence, although it still lurks in the shadow of her life. How has such a symptom been relegated from its position as a constant presence? Free associations broke through the "Johnny" and were allowed to contaminate the sterility between analyst and analysand. The welcoming of the mess of the dirty thought in the analytic situation made redundant the necessity for its warding off into a sterile or vomiting–anal world; a movement from a primitive mouth–anus bowel led an unconscious emotional life to one that is more bearable and to the possibility of enjoying the mess of ordinary human relationships.

Another female patient was born to a young mother of fifteen. Away from home, her teenage mother probably used the baby as a protective device against a much older husband and the adult world, as something to cling on to. Over time, the mother had become more paranoid and did not want her daughter to grow up and separate from her. She tried to follow her to university in another city, and since then had incessantly phoned and tried to visit many times a week. This form of terrorism against the daughter led to the development, in Ferenczi's term, of a "wise baby", who, from early on, mothered her mother, as she knew the mother was incapable of much adult functioning. Since analysis, the patient has been able to put up a much greater barrier to mother's huge intrusiveness. Instead of being in an oppositional state to mother's desired control, the patient has been more thoughtful and creative in the development of her own life.

Yet, there is a subtle somatic symptom. Despite being very keen on analysis, attending five times a week, making much use of the work and thinking it has saved her life, the patient lies nearly totally rigid on the couch. It is rare for her to move during the fifty minutes. Despite the intellectual strides that have been made, this points to a psychosomatic expression of her great unconscious anxiety: "I had better not move a muscle because mother will see and want to envelop me further", and/or "If I do not move I will stay hidden from her".

Recently, the patient has been able to question her capacity to appear to get what she wants in life. In job interviews and among colleagues, she seems to charm others into agreeing with her ideas. Indeed, she has been able to develop an intelligence that allows her to better organise her world, but with the unconscious expectation always that the metaphor of the mother returning to possess her is always hovering near. To the onlooker, the patient would appear much improved, perhaps nearing the end of a good analysis. I disagree, as the shadow of the mother had been skilfully suppressed from view and yet is so clearly visible in the psychosomatics of the patient lying on the couch, unmoving. There is more work to do.

A middle-aged homosexual man came to analysis because he had a failing relationship with an exceedingly demanding and much younger lover. It was soon apparent that he lived his intimate relationships in a sado-masochistic bind. Similarly, he was failing in his work and was enraged at how he was unable to speak up to colleagues and at meetings, despite realising that he had good things to say. He was describing a reluctance to really engage with his life.

In time, he moved from the telling of the facts of his life to speaking about things, to realising that he had not spoken about sex. He began to dare to talk of the constant need to have poor, younger, out of work, foreign partners. Ostensibly, he was the older, more mature, richer house owner, who could be father to the younger men. He went further and dared to reveal his massive anxiety at the moment of bodily intimacy when both would become naked. His life was fixed on avoiding this in all manner of ways. He feared that his penis was too small. Always the imaging was that the fitter young men were larger, and he could only balance the bodily discrepancy by being the older, richer man able to look after "the young cock".

This was a revelation, where, to his surprise, he did not feel humiliated. The expected dyad of one big person and one small person did not appear in the clinical setting. Instead, his free association was in the spirit of the equality of dialogue between analyst and analysand. This had a very different resonance from the usual sado-masochistic expectation of his fixed relationships. Over the next few months, with firm kindness, he got rid of the younger man, who, he now realised, was a somewhat nasty and demanding cuckoo in his nest. He found he could speak more freely at work, realised he was listened to, and became significantly promoted. The idea of a lover commensurate with his own age and achievements, on a level with him, began to interest him much more.

It is not known what size his organ actually is, flaccid or erect, but his imagination of its potency has certainly changed. The change has come about clinically by becoming able to free associate and realising that the clinical dyad was functioning in a concerned listening way, so different from the fixed paranoia of big and little.

A young man presented in analysis with much anxiety, consisting of constantly asking questions. He demanded reassurance, especially about his own self-diagnosis of an incipient psychosis. He constantly moved on the couch and preferred similarly constant mental movement, not settling into one topic on his mind but delving into too many. In a sense, his analysis was almost a total resistance to authentic free association. He had a history of the father walking out of the family when he was eight years old. But the story is told as if he had already adjusted his understanding of this in his thought processes. It seemed that he saw the task of analysis to be getting to know more and more about the analyst and, in particular, to try to pin down my analytic attitudes, especially regarding his expectation of my diagnosis of him. Not indulging him with answers and assurance was treated with caustic disdain and he continued to start and end sessions with questions. Without knowing much of the meaning of all this, it certainly had the quality of an attack on myself and the analytic work, as well as an intensity of antagonism from the beginning of analysis.

I did understand that the patient had hardly spoken in any depth about his life or history. The present tense of his difficulties seemed much more alluring and seemed to be the definition of his expectation of the work of analysis.

On several occasions, I interpreted not just his disinterest in his historical life, but how he was intent on keeping up a constant movement of evasion and to remaining with his questions in the present. In one session, he began with a dream fragment of suede shoes. He remembered that his mother had recently wanted him to have a suede jacket. Mother gave to him continuously and he took continuously from her. Again, his preference was to be in present time, and I interpreted this in an attempt to block the usual easy path of his resistance. To his own surprise, he then said, "There was something very wrong with my legs when I was born." He remembered that he needed to be in a fixed harness, like some kind of callipers, for many months so that the defect could mend. He began to think about what he was saying. He realised that although it had been in the first few months or year or two of his life, it was also an extremely potent metaphor of his intense hatred of any sense of restriction. As an infant, he had struggled to move, but it was impossible. Eventually, he would go very still and watch, only moving his eyes. He further associated that his mother had had a stillbirth prior to becoming pregnant with him. This had, apparently, led her to being in bed "for nine months of the pregnancy, not moving". Here, we see an even greater atmosphere of severe and actual restriction. The patient had a thoughtful realisation of the importance of the freedom of thinking and remembering that he was offering to both of us.

The constant psychical and mental movements he had been displaying on the couch and in his life could now begin to be understood as an almost total psychosomatisation of a fixed rigidity in his body harnessed in leg callipers to prevent movement. Not only was the mother rigid in fear for her unborn baby, but also her born baby was not able to move, despite initially struggling. He could watch with immense frustration, and this made clearer his addiction to films and his preference of watching and imagining a filmic life for himself away from reality. He was constantly on the move as a defence against being trapped and immobilised. This, too, was his powerful unconscious fear of analysis, that he would be fixed like an insect pinned to the couch, unable to move again.

The suede shoes dream fragment is likely to contain a representation of his traumatic early life. The opposite of soft shoes is the hardness of callipers rigidly fixing his legs.

The patient brings his profound early trauma in his physical posture and constant movement on the couch. In addition, he brings his fear of being trapped again by trying to stay in the present tense of his life. Resistance to the analytic task of free association now becomes the royal road for the discovery of his huge psychosomatic disposition of his life.

The analytic task is for the patient to realise the depth of his early deprivation, his intense clinging to mother, his great anxiety to move from his fixed body and mind, together with the pain of such realisation. The departure of his father when he was eight now can be seen as a much later event, and one that can include a capacity to move perceivably to a more healthy mental space. His contempt for a leaving father, which he kept finding in the gaps between sessions, concealed his hatred of his unconscious perception of mother pinning him down. This operated together with an intense fear that if he moved away from the mother's control, he might damage himself too much and be fixed, alone and unable to move—a position he must have constantly endured when mother was out of his gaze.

Discussion

Near the end of his *Diary*, Ferenczi writes about the need for "a capacity to integrate the fragments intellectually, there must also be kindness, as this alone makes integration permanent" (Ferenczi, 1932, p. 207). This is undoubtedly a statement against the supremacy of an intellectual analysis alone. However, in some analytic communities, this might be more common, as analytic material is reshaped within the intelligence of a pertinent interpretation, as if the work is done. Freud shrewdly recognised the need for working through. For Ferenczi, this would converge with the necessity to include the body. After all, the body of the infant requires caring for in a good enough scenario—a physical holding that is sensitive without making an adult sexual demand on the body. The analyst certain of boundaries is able to include the body of the patient without the fear of it heralding movement towards assault and incest. There is, of course, a riposte to the attitude of clinical kindness. Again in the *Diary*, he writes,

I have finally come to realise that it is an unavoidable task of the analyst. Although he may behave as he will, he may take kindness and relaxation as far as he possibly can, the time will come when he will have to repeat with his own hands the act of murder previously perpetuated against the patient. (Ferenczi, 1932, p. 52)

This is a good reason why such work is so difficult for patient and analyst. In order to come closer to the early terrible experiences contained in the body, enough of a relaxation in the body is required: this would become the physical territory of Groddeck in his Baden Baden spa. However, that in itself will not be sufficient, as the act of trauma needs to be discovered in the transference–countertransference in order for it to be defused and elevated from its binding in the body to a safe passage into emotional language in the clinical dyad. For the first clinical case, the patient knowing me as a contraceptive in order to prevent the birth of some deeper emotionality is an example of an act of murder in the transference, signifying, in all likelihood, the mother's attempt to abort her daughter.

In this chapter, there is a plea to take the body of the patient as seriously as the mind and language. As Ferenczi eloquently remarked, "one needs to have lived through an affective experience, to have, so to speak, felt it in one's body, in order to gain conviction" (Ferenczi, 1912, p. 194).

Several hospital departments had seen a patient, as his buttock pain was unswerving in its intense chronicity. No medicine had any effect. Eventually the specialist Pain Clinic referred him for a psychodynamic interview. For the first time he was asked what was happening in his life at the onset of symptoms. The instant reply was that he was attending his father's funeral. At once the free association spoke: "My father was such a pain in the arse." The aftermath of such a revelation was that although the pain was not instantly made to vanish, the patient, knowing its history, became much less concerned. In a way, he had no need to continue searching in hospitals for the completion of his mourning.

To return to the beginning, Appelfeld was pitched into a nightmare world without kindness. If the body is to be reclaimed from the clutches of deep defences, a relationship that recognises and revives the traumatic position in order to develop growth from a bodily regression is essential.

References

Ferenczi, S. (1912). Transitory symptom-constructions during the analysis. In: *First Contributions to the Problems and Methods of Psycho-Analysis* (pp. 193–212). London: Hogarth Press, 1952 [reprinted, London: Karnac, 1994].

Ferenczi, S. (1932). *The Clinical Diary of Sándor Ferenczi*, J. Dupont (Ed.), M. Balint & N. Z. Jackson (Trans.). Cambridge, MA: Harvard University Press, 1988.

CHAPTER THIRTEEN

Close to the body: an analyst's daily work with cancer patients

Ágnes Riskó

T his chapter is a result of my experiences at the National Institute of Oncology in Budapest. Since 1990, I have worked as a psychoanalyst with an oncohaematology team. I treat in-patients and outpatients suffering from malignant lymphomas with psychoanalytical psychotherapy, and treat some survivors with psychoanalysis.

When I began to work at the oncohaematology department, my medical oncologist colleague, Tamás Fleischmann, noted that oncology is a difficult field for psychologists and psychiatrists. They find working with cancer patients complicated; it is easy to get lost because there are no well-beaten paths of treatment for them to follow. I would like to talk about some of my observations at the oncohaematology department—observations concerning cancer patients undergoing oncological treatment, medical doctors and nurses, and the main psychoanalytical experience gained from our common work.

Entering any oncology department, you can feel that somehow every phenomenon, event, and act is in a very deep connection with the body, with the body-ego, or (after Ferenczi) with the "archaic part" of the personality (Ferenczi, 1955). The cause of these special psychic processes and this atmosphere is the sudden and overwhelming bodily and psychic crisis evoked by learning of the diagnosis of cancer. As Balint wrote (1957), the cancer disease represents the basic fault and the fearful inner "bad", which attacks and fills the diseased person from the inside with oral aggressiveness. That is the main reason for the patients' anxiety—especially their growing death-anxiety—and psychic regression, which are independent from their actual knowledge about the chances for recovery.

The first impressions of the oncology department are the following: the hospital and the department are separated from the "outside world"; the specialists' language and uniforms are uncommon. One readily feels the unusual silence, the distinctive smell, the non-transparent congestion in consequence of projected "bad" objects, the patients' special handling of time and space, the intuition of the split communication—verbal and non-verbal "messages" are disintegrated—between patients and staff members. The unconscious activity of projective identification by patients, relatives, and specialists breaks through the barriers separating the people like the expansion of a tumour in the body. This mental mechanism, the projective identification, binds the patients to specialists, and everybody can feel the pressure to contain their emotions. On the oncological ward, everybody is "in the same boat": through projective identification, everybody has a permanent influence on everyone else. This process overwhelms bodies, souls, the atmosphere, and the way of thinking, causing radical and sudden changes in time experience, in orientation, in reality testing, and in emotional and cognitive functioning. These are the reasons why, unexpectedly and for shorter or longer periods, the ill adolescents and adults become children/infants again and their repressed early traumas might again be activated. We often recognise the patients' psychic burden because of their psychic regression to a paranoid–schizoid position, as described by Melanie Klein. The complex regression of certain cancer patients has two strata—the early, repressed and reactivated psychic traumas and symptoms, and the signs of acute psychic and bodily shock in connection to those traumas. My supervisor, István Székács-Schönberger noted: "It's a wonder that these patients are conscious!"

Let us consider the complex status of cancer patients who are under active oncological treatment. The cancer patients are afraid of external and internal dangers. The external dangers are the unexpected, dreadful illness itself, the learning of the certain diagnosis and the uncertain prognosis, the fearsome examinations and treatments, the radical and previously unimaginable—even if transitory— changes of their body and bodily functioning, such as being bald and pale, feeling unwell all the time, losing fertility, being dependent, etc. The internal dangers are, before effective onco-treatment, the imminent multiplication of the cancer cells, which makes obvious the inner "bad" and chaos. Once treatment begins, there is fear of the repeated destructive effects of chemo- and radiotherapy, and the loss of control of their bodily functions (which is connected with psychic control).

I apply projective tests (Rorschach, Szondi) during my work to try to learn more about the inner world of our patients. It is probable that a lot of cancer patients have serious difficulty expressing verbally their special concerns and feelings, their anxiety concerning inhibition of ego-functions, craving for attachment, rage, guilt, panic, fear of their anguished body, fear of loss of control, urge for suicide, etc. Therefore, strong, archaic psychic defence mechanisms emerge which are recognisable, such as projection, denial, etc. The patients are able to speak directly of their strong envy. Often they tell me: I envy the healthy colour of your skin, I would like to swop our arms, your arms seem to me wiry, could we also swop our legs? I envy your strength, like a foetus I want nourishment from your vitality. I need your vitality! I would like to slip into your body and get your inner content. After discussing the results of projective tests, the above-mentioned colleague, Tamás Fleischmann, remarked, "I had a lot of impressions about the serious psychic problems of our patients, about their extreme situation, but these results are worse than I imagined."

Now, some words about medical doctors and nurses. The psychoanalyst Donald Winnicott said, "There is no such thing as an infant, only mother and infant together" (1965). Especially in the field of oncology, we can relate that there is no such thing as a patient, only a patient and his/her therapist (medical doctor, nurse, clinical psychologist, psychiatrist, etc.) together. I know from experience that other hospital staff and that the relatives of patients belong closely to the patients as well.

At our department, the patients are treated with chemotherapy. The patients label the infusion differently: poison, toxin, spray insecticide, or mother's milk, manna from heaven, soft drink. It is not difficult to conclude from the patient's label the not completely unconscious attitude of the patient toward the therapist: very often the

Self portrait I, by PN, a patient suffering from malignant lymphoma.

regressed, disturbed patients consider their therapist as a persecutor ("terminator", Mengele) or as a good-enough mother.

From my experience, the staff working closely with these patients frequently try to minimise patient contact (verbal and non-verbal), especially with incurable, highly disturbed cancer patients, because these patients might have a significant effect on their own emotional and physical stability and professional self-esteem. In the counter-transference, the therapists might experience "coenesthetic empathy" (Spitz, 1965, p. 134): bodily identification, psychosomatic symptoms,

Self portrait II, painted one month later by PN.

exhaustion, discouragement, anger, humiliation, and a wish to get rid of the patient.

As I mentioned above, we can observe that each staff member becomes an "unconscious container". A physiotherapist described her self-monitoring: "Treating cancer patients I feel as if I were a balloon, which is getting bigger and bigger. I practically feel how the tension is increasing inside my body. I cannot do anything to reduce it. When the last patient leaves I feel deflated as if I were pricked with a pin. I am tired, especially mentally. It is hard to get over it, sometimes it is impossible." My colleague's comment shows that because of the tension of "bad" objects, the closeness of the imagined impending death, and the influence of aggressive oncological therapies, the psychic state of patients is often such that they are in a fluctuating, borderline-like psychic regression without borderline personality disorder. The medical doctors and nurses are not prepared for the empathic handling of the patients' frequently hidden psychic problems and symptoms; as a result, especially those working without supervision experience guilt, relevant powerlessness, and burn-out symptoms. At the beginning of my work in the oncohaematology department, I usually treated patients; later, I discovered the psychic burden carried by the relatives. Now, more and more, I try to help my colleagues and the patients' relatives.

As Reatto (2004) said, we need to realise that the oncology staff members also are exposed to the patient's primitive anxiety and projection. The specialists might respond with (usually repressed) feelings of helplessness, despair, or, conversely, with omnipotent wishes, which can result in a mechanical and cold attitude, supported by the available technology. Here, too, the psychoanalyst can provide a useful contribution by making available to the medical staff the opportunity to work on their possible countertransference reactions, with the help of individual counselling or more psychoanalytical psychotherapy or psychoanalysis.

To close my chapter, I would like to talk about the so-called irregular, intensive supervision with my training analyst, István Székács-Schönberger. In 1991, we discussed our joint interest in oncopsychology, and undertook to try to understand and name the phenomena and events that were experienced in the oncology department. We focused on dream-work. During the long supervision, we talked about the non-verbal (acoustic, visual, odour, and touch manifestations) and verbal experiences, which were analysed by discussion of the transference and countertransference. On oncology wards, the process of transfer is natural (as Ferenczi said) and very intensive, and the countertransference is more complex than on other wards. So, intensive supervision is essential because of the increased psychic load and the rather unknown depths of psychoanalytical oncopsychology.

The work as a team member psychoanalyst on the oncohaematology ward—the psychoanalytical psychotherapy and psychoanalysis of cancer patients—can be regarded as "close to the body" psycho-analysis, based on the traditions of the Budapest School.

References

Balint, M. (1957). *The Doctor, His Patient and The Illness*. New York: International Universities Press.

Ferenczi, S. (1955). *Final Contributions to the Problems and Methods of Psycho-Analysis*, M. Balint (Ed.), E. Mosbacher & others (Trans.). London: Hogarth Press, 1955 [reprinted, London: Karnac, 1994].

Reatto, L. (2004). The subjective experience of illness and the therapeutic process: being a psychoanalyst in oncology. Lecture in Budapest, 26 February 2004.

Spitz, R. A. (1965). *The First Year of My Life*. New York: International University Press.

Winnicott, D. W. (1965). *The Maturational Processes and the Facilitating Environment*. London: Hogarth Press.

CHAPTER FOURTEEN

"Poor Konrad": the body and the soul seekers[1]

Ferenc Erős

I n a letter dated 27 April 1910, Sandor Ferenczi reacted with embarrassment to Freud's suggestion to invite Abraham Brill to their planned common vacation in Sicily. Ferenczi was far from happy about this plan, which, as he wrote, "immediately aroused my slumbering brother complex" (Ferenczi, 1910, p. 167). He continues:

> I can't raise any objection to the invitation other than the unjustified infantile desire to be the first and only one with the 'father'. I like Brill very much and [am] *in complete agreement* that you should invite him. But between the two suggested modalities I would still like to choose the one that states the three of us make only *a part* of the journey. That is not only a small concession to my complexes (which I usually handle as badly as Spitteler does his 'poor Konrad'), but also has its logical foundation. There are questions (of both personal and scientific nature) which we can settle much more economically alone than in Brill's presence; these should also get their due. (Ferenczi, 1910, p. 167)

Who is Spitteler and who is his "poor Konrad"? "Poor Konrad" is none other than the physical body, a nickname used by the hero, the poet Viktor, for his own body in a novel entitled *Imago* that was published in 1906 by the Swiss–German novelist, poet, and essayist

Carl Spitteler (1845–1924).[2] Spitteler's name perhaps sounds less familiar nowadays, but he was a celebrated writer of his age—he received the Nobel Prize in 1919. The prize was donated as an acknowledgment of his outstanding literary achievement as well as his pacifism—a political gesture, just after the Second World War, toward his country, neutral Switzerland. Although, like Gottfried Keller and Conrad Ferdinand Meyer, he was regarded as a character-istic figure of modern Swiss German literature at the time, he is almost forgotten today, perhaps because his heavily romantic, mythological language makes his works difficult to read.

Nevertheless, at least one work, his novel *Imago* survived its author. In addition to its literary values, this work has a particular significance in the history of psychoanalysis. The immortality of the *title* of the book itself is granted by the fact that, in 1912, the name *Imago* was chosen for the first journal that aimed at a combination of psychoanalysis and the human sciences (*Geisteswissenschaften*). The idea to name the new journal after Spitteler's novel came from Hanns Sachs, who founded and co-edited *Imago* with Otto Rank, and who published several essays and commentaries on this highly respected Swiss author in their journal (Sachs, 1913, 1924, 1935). *American Imago*, founded by Sigmund Freud and Hanns Sachs in 1939, perpetuated the spirit of Spitteler's novel for our time.

Carl Spitteler.

But it was not only the title itself that made an impact. The key novel, *Imago*, as well as some other works of the Swiss master, were widely read and even admired in psychoanalytic circles in the early twentieth century. Most notably, Spitteler's other famous Swiss compatriot, Carl Gustav Jung, derived his own notion of "imago" from this novel (Jung, 1972, p. 299); moreover, he devoted a whole chapter to Spitteler in his major typological work, under the title "The problem of types in poetry," where he discusses Spitteler's epic poem *Prometheus and Epimetheus* (Jung, 1930). Georg Groddeck, the father of psychosomatics, and the author of *The Book of the Id* and the key psychoanalytic novel *The Soul Seeker* (Der Seelensucher), wrote in 1905, one year before the publication of the novel, *Imago*, an enthusiastic review of *Olympic Spring* (Der olympische Frühling, 1900–1905), another epic poem by the Swiss writer.

Frontispice of Spitteler's *Imago*, 1906.

It was mostly Jung and Sachs who popularised Spitteler's cult, but Freud also made a number of references to the Swiss author in *The Interpretation of Dreams* and in other places. Re-reading Spitteler today, one might wonder why psychoanalysts found his works so attractive, in spite of the fact that their feelings were not returned by Spitteler. According to Hanns Sachs, the Swiss writer despised psychoanalysis and called it "a horrifying scientific Esperanto that one has to translate first to plain German" (Sachs, 1924).

Paradoxically, it appears that his blank refusal of psychoanalysis only enhanced his cult among analysts. Freud, in a footnote added to Chapter IV in the later editions of *The Interpretation of Dreams*, notes:

> A great contemporary poet, who, I am told, will hear nothing of psycho-analysis and dream-interpretation, has nevertheless derived from his own experience an almost identical formula for the nature of the dream: 'Unauthorized emergence of suppressed yearnings under false features and names'. (Freud, 1900a, p. 160, n.1, footnote added 1914)

Freud refers here to Spitteler's early childhood recollections (*Meine frühesten Erlebnisse*), published in 1914 (Spitteler, 1914).

Hanns Sachs' *Übermensch*-like admiration of Spitteler went so far that he saw in the poet "the kind of superiority produced by special gifts that fall mysteriously from the laps of the gods". He described their contact with the following words:

> Carl Spitteler whom I visited several times when I came to Lucerne was duly flattered by becoming godfather of a scientific journal, but not at all interested in a systematic disquisition about the nature of the unconscious. He shrank instinctively from anything that could disrupt his artistic intuition. (Sachs, 1945, quoted in Plank, 1953, p. 392)

Antal Szerb, a Hungarian writer and essayist of the 1930s, came to a similar conclusion. In his scholarly overview of world literature, he notes ironically of Spitteler that: "... he spent his whole long life in the ascetic service of the Work of Art" (Szerb, 1962, p. 758).

Thus, Spitteler *himself* did not like psychoanalysis, but psychoanalysts *adored him*. This may have been because his style and language, and the mood and the themes represented by Spitteler, fit perfectly the literary taste of the self-critical *Bildungsbürgertum*, that educated *fin de siècle* bourgeoisie to which, among other psychoanalysts of the age, Freud, Jung, and Ferenczi belonged. These people despised the morals of the bourgeois world of which they were part and parcel. Artistic (and also scientific) creativity was, for them, an imaginary way out from—using Spitteler's term—"the hell of conviviality [*Gemütlichkeit*]" (Spitteler, 1942, p. 65). Spitteler's mystical and symbolic mythological language, his intimacy, his late romantic rhetoric coupled with bitter irony and sometimes with an astonishing naturalism, as well as his preoccupation with dreams, dreamlike phantasies, and delusions, fully opened his work to psychoanalytic interpretation and imagination. Or, to put it in another way, a *common space* was created for psychoanalysis and literature. Freud's early interest in the sources of artistic inspiration and creativity in art, "Creative writers and daydreaming", *Leonardo da Vinci*, and, most notably, his essay on the work of another German writer, *Gradiva*, by Wilhelm Jensen (which was born in a spiritual exchange with Carl Gustav Jung) demonstrate the existence of such a common space or a discursive community of interpretations between writers and psychoanalysts.

These two exemplary novels, Jensen's *Gradiva* and Spitteler's *Imago*, have many common features, in as much as the heroes of both works were deluded and captured by an imago, by an imaginary woman, *das ewig Weibliche*, "the eternal feminine", in Goethe's sense. The ideal woman is contrasted to the earthly appearance and meanness of the same woman. In Spitteler's novel, this imago is represented by a "Severe Lady", as the poet Viktor, the hero of the novel, calls her in his phantasies. She is a lady named Theuda, who appears to the poet in everyday life, in the "hell of conviviality", as "Pseuda", that is, the "false" or the "liar". Norbert Hanold, the archaeologist, and Viktor, the poet are both "soul seekers", as well as Thomas Weltlein, the hero of Groddeck's *Der Seelensucher* (The Soul Seeker) (1921).[3] The "soul seeking" type of work was, of course, a characteristic genre in the early twentieth century European literature—from Arthur Schnitzler and Stefan Zweig to Thomas Mann, Romain Rolland, and Marcel Proust.

Let me refer briefly to a Hungarian novel, the aforementioned Antal Szerb's *Journey by Moonlight* (2000), first published in 1937. This work was cult reading for my generation in the 1960s and is still very popular in Hungary. It was, however, unknown outside Hungary until its recent publication in German, English, Italian, Spanish,

Portuguese, and other languages. It has now obtained a belated international reputation. The book is about a young Hungarian, Mihály's
real journey throughout Italy, and his imaginary journey into his own
soul. His journey is a despaired attempt at escape from the "hell of
conviviality". In pursuit of his own Imago, his secret adolescent love,
Éva Ulpius, Mihály abandons his wife, Erzsi, on the train between
Florence and Rome. The two main female figures of Szerb's novel
represent a similar split to the one we find in Spitteler's *Imago* between
Theuda and Pseuda, that is to say, between the heavenly and the
earthly woman.

In contrast to Spitteler, Szerb was not untrained in, or hostile to,
psychoanalysis. Quite the contrary, he was fully aware of the importance of psychoanalysis, and he wrote a genuine psychoanalytic novel
richly decorated with such themes as sibling love, Oedipal rivalry,
homosexual desire, and so on. Nevertheless, he often takes an ironic
stance toward psychoanalysis. As one of the novel's characters, a
Hungarian professor of archaeology in Rome explains to Mihály:

> "I really detest those people who like to draw practical conclusions
> from scholarly truth, who apply learning 'to real life,' like engineers
> who turn the propositions of chemistry into insecticides for bedbugs.
> It translates, in Goethe's words, as 'life is gray, but the golden tree of
> theory is always green.' Especially when itself is as green as it is. Now
> I hope I've restored your equilibrium. Here is a general rule . . . don't
> try to live the life of the soul. I think that's your problem. An intelli-
> gent person doesn't have a spiritual life." (Szerb, 2000, p. 161)

But let us go back to Spitteler and his "poor Konrad". The expression is well known in German history: "poor Konrad" (*der arme
Konrad*) was the name of a peasants' alliance (the *Bundschuch*) that
launched an uprising in Württemberg in 1514 as an antecedent of the
great German peasant wars in Luther's age. The uprising of the "poor
Konrad" was, in a certain sense, a "revolt of the body", ridden by
misery, need, hunger, and powerlessness. It must also be noted that
Spitteler had published another novel where the name Konrad
appeared: *Conrad, der Leutnant* (1898). This was, in essence, a natural-
istic description of an Oedipal father–son conflict ending in the
murder of the father.

In the beginning of the novel *Imago*, Viktor, Spitteler's hero, also
a late reincarnation of Goethe's young Werther, seems to be in an

"intimate friendship" with "poor Konrad". But, as the story advances, and the contrast between the heavenly Theuda and the earthly Pseuda becomes more and more unbearable, "poor Konrad" intervenes and warns his "Master": "I am also here" (Spitteler, 1942, p. 34). Thus, the once intimate friend changes into a dreadful enemy, a traitor. In Spitteler's perfectly "Jungian" novel, Imago represents *Anima*, Reason represents Animus, and "poor Konrad" would be equivalent to the *Shadow*. "Poor Konrad" is also the *Doppelgänger,* the "double", so familiar from Adalbert Chamisso's *Peter Schlemihl* or E. T. A. Hoffmann's *The Devil's Elixir*. The "double" was "the main spectre of German romanticism", as Antal Szerb, the author of *Journey by Moonlight*, notes in his work on world literature, mentioned above (Szerb, 1962, p. 758).

Freud, in his essay on The "uncanny" (1919h) speaks about the uncanny effect of the double, the effect of suddenly and unexpectedly meeting with one's own image: for example, meeting with the image of our own body in a mirror. Jacques Lacan further elaborated this theme in his concept of the "mirror stage", and it also concerns the Lacanian notion of the Real (*le réel*), in which the body, in its brute physicality, is opposed to its symbolic and imaginary functions (Lacan, 1977; see also Evans, 1996). Returning to Spitteler, the main source of his own representation of body goes back to his master Nietzsche, who uses the body as a *metaphor of intellect*, a text which must be deciphered as a signifier of power and will (Faulkner, 2003).

However tempting it would be to discuss the philosophical and, first of all, Nietzschean context of Spitteler's *oeuvre*, let us see now how and in which contexts "poor Konrad" appears in the Freud–Ferenczi correspondence. Certainly, it should have been a frequently used figure of speech among psychoanalysts; the expression appears first in the correspondence between Freud and Jung. I have already quoted Ferenczi's letter of 27 April 1910, arguing against inviting Brill to the Sicilian vacation, which was such an important landmark in the development of the relationship between Freud and Ferenczi. Let us see now how Freud reports on the common trip with Ferenczi to Jung:

> The first week on the island was delightful, the second, because of the continuous sirocco, a hard trial for poor Konrad. Now at least we feel that we have come through it all: the sirocco and threat of cholera and malaria. . . . My travelling companion is a dear fellow, but dreamy in

a disturbing kind of way, and his attitude toward me is infantile. He never stops admiring me, which I don't like, and is probably sharply critical of me in his unconscious when I am taking it easy. He has been too passive and receptive. Letting everything be done for him like a woman, and I haven't got enough homosexuality in me to accept him as one. These trips arouse a great longing for a real woman . . . (Freud, 1910a, p. 353)

It is interesting to compare the above letter with the one Freud wrote to Ferenczi a few days later, on 6 October 1910.

Not only have you noticed that I no *longer* have any need for that full opening of my personality, but you have also understood it and correctly returned it to its traumatic cause. Why did you thus make a point of it? This need has been extinguished in me since Fliess's case, with the overcoming of which you just saw me occupied. A piece of homosexual investment has been withdrawn and utilized for the enlargement of my own ego. I have succeeded where the paranoiac falls. Add[ed] to this is the fact that I was for the most part not very well, I suffered more from my intestinal troubles than I cared to admit. And I often said to myself: he who is not master of his Konrad should not travel. The honesty should have begun there, and you didn't seem stable enough not to become overconcerned. (Freud, 1910b, pp. 221–222)

"Poor Konrad" turns up again in a letter dated on 3 November 1912. On this day Ferenczi wrote to Freud,

I must also still report about my poor Konrad. The weight loss (five kilograms) and general fatigue is probably the reason for the fact that my heart is also not behaving quite properly. Dr. Lévy, a *very* reliable internist can't find any organic change, only a 'laziness' of the left ventricle. . . . Locally (right inguinal glands) still *some* sensitivity to pain, otherwise everything back to normal. (Ferenczi, 1912, p. 426)

In the 1910 letter, Ferenczi uses "poor Konrad" as a metaphor for his complexes, in self-analysing his resistance to welcoming Brill as partner for a vacation in Sicily. In this letter, the reference to Spitteler's novel creates an ironic and playful distance between his own person and his bodily states. He is like the conscientious doctor who examines and cares for his own body as he would for anyone else's, and narrates his symptoms to Freud quite accurately and objectively (even though Freud is reluctant to take them seriously).

We should not forget, however, that this letter was written in the period of the height of the crisis with two women, Gizella and Elma, mother and daughter. Ferenczi's detailed accounts of his real or imagined bodily symptoms, together with the detailed and extremely sincere accounts of his dreams, phantasies, associations, and feelings are all "materials" offered to the attention of Freud as a virtual analyst. "Poor Konrad" appears here, translated into the discourse of Spitteler's characters, as victim of the internal fight between Theuda, the ideal woman, and her earthly appearance, Pseuda. In the correspondence, we can follow to the end how painful this split was for Ferenczi. Nine years later, in his letter to Freud on 16 May 1921, Ferenczi warns with the following words, "You must finally, once and for all, be considerate of your 'poor Konrad'" (Ferenczi, 1921, p. 57). While in the first two quotations Ferenczi speaks of his own "poor Konrad", now the main concern becomes that of Freud's. This remarkable shift from "my" to "your" sheds light on the significance of body in their relationship as well as in the development of Ferenczi's conceptions of trauma and mutual analysis.

Space limits do not allow me to go into further details of the Freud–Ferenczi relationship that has received so much attention in recent publications (Haynal, 2002). I have tried to point out only those places in the correspondence where the quoted references to "poor Konrad" seem to play a crucial role. All these have, of course, further and far-leading implications. I can mention only a few of these here.

1. The problem of the body has a central role in Ferenczi's theory of trauma. The "corporal return of the trauma" might take the form of the mimetic incorporation of the thoughts and feelings of the aggressor. In this sense, body is a text that can be read; it is a surface on which the external world, the interpersonal and institutional power relations, leave their marks. Much later, Michel Foucault elaborated this topic in his genealogical works.[4] According to the German psychoanalyst and sociologist, Alfred Lorenzer, the basic tenet of all psychoanalytic knowledge is the *bodily* *"inscription"*, the inscription of sense—of a social sense—into the body. The fact that the contents of experience are related to the body (*Leib*) is *the* distinctive feature of Freudian psychology:

psychoanalysis as a science deals with the social imprint on nature and the natural imprint on the social (Lorenzer, 2002).

2.   Ferenczi can be regarded—together with Spitteler, Groddeck, one of the great soul seekers, and others—as a pioneer of psycho-analytic psychosomatics, that emphasises the role of psychical sources (such as regression and narcissism) in the origin of organic diseases and physical injuries. In the genealogy of Ferenczi's concept of psychosomatics, "my poor Konrad", that is, Ferenczi's *own* psychosomatic symptoms, and "your poor Konrad", that is, *Freud's* psychosomatic symptoms, may deserve special attention. It seems that not only Imago, but its counter-part, "poor Konrad", made a career that the Swiss writer, half-forgotten today, had never dreamt of.

3.   The problem of the body emerges as one of the most important aspects of Ferenczi's work. Because he was a physician by train-ing and attitude, it was only natural for him that he regarded "body" as a physical object, part of Nature both in its growth and decay. However, because he was a psychoanalyst, it was also natural for him to regard the body and its symptoms as part of the psychic reality, a *text* in which each part and organ of the body has a symbolic meaning. Nietzsche's spirit returns on the pages of Ferenczi's *Clinical Diary*: "In such moments when the psychic system fails, the organism begins to think" (Ferenczi, 1932, p. 6). Thus, the ailing and fragile figure of "poor Konrad" attains immortality. "Soul seeking" has achieved its goal.

To sum up, Spitteler's *unintentional* contribution to the history of psychoanalysis, his novel *Imago* and the creation of "poor Konrad's" metaphor in it, helped early psychoanalysts Jung, Freud, and Ferenczi to formulate their own bodily feelings in a discursive, intersubjective form. Beyond its personal, biographical significance, the metaphor received theoretical importance, too, in the Freud–Ferenczi corre-spondence.

Notes

1.   Ths chapter is based on a paper presented to the 24th International Literature and Psychology Conference, University of Belgrade, Serbia,

July 4–9, 2007, which itself is a revised and extended version of the paper originally prepared for CONFERENCZI – Hungarian Psychoanalytic Ideas Revisited, a conference organised by IMAGO MLPC and the Freud Museum, London, April 23–25, 2004. This chapter was originally published in A. Dimitrijevic, E. M. Fox, & M. M. Schwartz (Eds.), *Psychoanalytic Encounters: Interdisciplinary Papers in Applied Psychoanalysis* (pp. 123–132). Belgrade: University of Belgrade, Faculty of Philosophy, 2010.

2. I am using the Hungarian translation (Spitteler, 1942). See also the fragmentary French translation: Spitteler, 1979. As far as I know, Spitteler's novel has never been translated into English.

3. The original title of the novel was "Der Wanzentöter oder die entschleierte Seele Thomas Weltleins" (The bug killer or the disguised soul of Thomas Weltlein).

4. On the concept of the body in Nietzsche and Foucault, see Csabai and Erős, 2000; Featherstone, Hepworth, and Turner, 1995; Huter, 1994.

References

Csabai, M., & Erős, F. (2000). *Testhatárok és énhatárok* (Borders of the Body and Borders of the Self). Budapest: Jószöveg.

Evans, D. (1996). *An Introductory Dictionary of Lacanian Psychoanalysis.* London: Routledge.

Faulkner, J. (2003). The body as text in the writings of Nietzsche and Freud. *Minerva. An Internet Journal of Philosophy,* 7: 2003. Available at: www.ul.ie/~philos/vol7/body.html.

Featherstone, M., Hepworth, M., & Turner, B. S. (Eds.) (1995). *The Body. Social Process and Cultural Theory.* London: Sage.

Ferenczi, S. (1910). Letter from Sándor Ferenczi to Sigmund Freud, April 27, 1910. In: E. Brabant, E. Falzeder, & P. Giampieri-Deutsch (Eds.), *The Correspondence of Sigmund Freud and Sándor Ferenczi Volume 1, 1908–1914* (pp. 167–168). Cambridge, MA: Harvard University Press, 1993.

Ferenczi, S. (1912). Letter from Sándor Ferenczi to Sigmund Freud, November 3, 1912. In: E. Brabant, E. Falzeder, & P. Giampieri-Deutsch (Eds.), *The Correspondence of Sigmund Freud and Sándor Ferenczi Volume 1, 1908–1914* (pp. 425–427), Harvard University Press, Cambridge, MA, 1993

Ferenczi, S. (1921). Letter from Sándor Ferenczi to Sigmund Freud, May 16, 1921. In: E. Falzeder & E. Brabant (Eds.), *The Correspondence of*

Sigmund Freud and Sándor Ferenczi Volume 3, 1920–1933 (pp. 56–58)
Harvard University Press, Cambridge, MA, 2000.

Ferenczi, S. (1932). *The Clinical Diary of Sándor Ferenczi*, J. Dupont (Ed.),
M. Balint & N. Z. Jackson (Trans.). Cambridge, MA: Harvard University Press, 1988.

Freud, S. (1900a). *The Interpretation of Dreams* (First Part). *S.E.*, 4. London:
Hogarth.

Freud, S. (1910a). Letter from Sigmund Freud to C. G. Jung, September 24,
1910. In: W. McGuire (Ed.), *The Freud/Jung Letters: The Correspondence
Between Sigmund Freud and C. G. Jung* (pp. 353–355), Princeton
University Press, Princeton, 1994.

Freud, S. (1910b). Letter from Sigmund Freud to Sándor Ferenczi, October
6, 1910. In: E. Brabant, E. Falzeder, & P. Giampieri-Deutsch (Eds.), *The
Correspondence of Sigmund Freud and Sándor Ferenczi Volume 1, 1908–
1914* (pp. 221–223). Cambridge, MA: Harvard University Press, 1993.

Freud, S. (1919h). The "uncanny". *S.E.*, 17: pp. 217–256. London: Hogarth.

Groddeck, G. (1921). *Der Seelensucher. Ein psychoanalytischer Roman*. Vienna:
Internationaler Psychoanalytischer [reprinted Frankfurt: Stroemfeld,
1998].

Haynal, A. (2002). *Disappearing and Reviving. Sándor Ferenczi in the History
of Psychoanalysis*. London: Karnac.

Huter, M. (1994). Body as metaphor: aspects of the critique and crisis of
language at the turn of the century with reference to Egon Schiele. In:
P. Werkner (Ed.), *Egon Schiele. Art, Sexuality, and Viennese Modernism*
(pp. 119–130). Palo Alto, CA: The Society for the Promotion of Science
and Scholarship.

Jung, C. G. (1930). *Psychologische Typen*. Zurich: Rascher.

Jung, C. G. (1972). *Two Essays on Analytical Psychology*. Princeton, NJ:
Princeton University Press.

Lacan, J. (1977). The mirror stage as formative of the *I* function as revealed
in psychoanalytic experience, A. Sheridan (Trans.). In: *Ecrits: A
Selection* (pp. 3–9). New York: Norton.

Lorenzer, A. (2002). What is an "Unconscious phantasy"?, T. Schaffrik
(Trans.). In: T. Schaffrik, *The Work of Alfred Lorenzer* (Appendix 7.1).
Available at: http://bidok.uibk.ac.at/library/schaffrik-lorenzer-work
-e.html#id3279040.

Plank, E. N. (1953). Memories of early childhood in autobiographies.
Psychoanalytic Study of the Child, 8: 381–393.

Sachs, H. (1913). Carl Spitteler. *Imago*, 2: 73–77.

Sachs, H. (1924). Carl Spitteler. *Imago*, 10: 443–447.

Sachs, H. (1935). Spittelers Erdenfahrt. Bemerkungen zu Robert Faesi, Spittelers Weg und Werk. *Imago, 21*: 92–95.

Sachs, H. (1945). *Freud: Master and Friend*. Cambridge, MA: Harvard University Press.

Spitteler, C. (1906). *Imago*. Jena: Eugen Diederichs.

Spitteler, C. (1914). *Meine frühesten Erlebnisse* (My earliest Experiences). Jena: Eugen Diederichs [reprinted Zurich: Artemis & Winkler, 1986].

Spitteler, C. (1942). *Imago*, I. Hertelendy (Trans.). Budapest: Révai.

Spitteler, C. (1979). *Imago* [Excerpts in French], F. Samson & P. Thèves (Trans.). *Le Coq-Héron, 73* : 3–19.

Szerb, A. (1962). *A világirodalom története* (A History of World Literature). Budapest: Magvető.

Szerb, A. (2000). *Journey by Moonlight*, Len Rix (Trans.). London: Pushkin Press.

INDEX

affect, xxvi, 6, 30, 32, 34, 97, 119, 142–143, 149–150, 157
aggression, 36, 39–40, 50, 52, 137, 175
  impulses, 35–36
  oral, xix, 160
  philobatic, 83
  pleasurable, 36
Alexander, F., xxi, xxix–xxx
American Psychoanalytic Association (APA), xxxiii
Amery, J., 117
anxiety, 5–7, 13–14, 34, 78–80, 83, 86, 92–93, 98, 113, 135, 154, 156, 160–161
  castration, xxxv
  death-, 160
  intense, 113
  massive, 153
  ocnophile, 87
  primitive, 78, 164
  psychotic, 23
  unconscious, 22, 153
Anzieu, D., 86, 88–89
Aron, L., xxxvi–xxxvii
Ashbery, J., xxvi, xxxvii
attachment, 78, 110, 150, 161
  anaclictic, xxix
  modalities, 84
  theory, xxiv
Auschwitz, xix, 120, 130
Austro-Hungarian Compromise (*Ausgleich*), 8

Balbernie, R., xxx, xxxvii
Balint, A., xviii, 6, 59–60, 63, 65, 67–68, 71–75, 98
Balint, E., xviii, xxi–xxii, 59, 83, 89, 91, 93–95, 97–99
Balint, J., 65
Balint, M., xviii–xix, xxi–xxii, xxvii–xxix, xxxiv, xxxvii, 5–6, 10, 32, 41, 59, 61–63, 65–68, 71–75, 77–82, 84–85, 88–89, 91–92, 94–98, 160
Balint Groups, 95
Balint Society, 63
Beebe, B., xxx, xxxvii
behaviour(al), 20, 110, 113, 134, 174
  adult, 78
  analyst's, 62
  careful, 83
  child-like, 12
  creative, 15–16
  hateful, 131

  inconsistent, 15
  patterns, 107
  perverse, xxxiii
  scandalous, 113
Benedek, T., xxi, xxix
Berény, R., 70
Bergmann, M., 137, 143
Bergsmann, E., 71
Bolshevik
  revolution, xxxiv, 11
  terror, 11
Bonomi, C., 137–138, 143
Brabant, E., xxvi–xxvii, xxxvi–xxxvii
Brierley, M., 32, 41
Brill, A., 167, 173–174
British Independent Group, xxii, xxxi
British Object Relations
  School, 60
  theory, xxix, 5
British Psychoanalytical Society, xxxiii, 5, 32, 60, 97
British Psychological Society, xxvi
Bucci, W., xxx, xxxvii
Budapest Medical School, xxxiv, 67
Budapest School of Psychoanalysis, xxi–xxiii, xxxi, 6, 165

Caillois, R., 78–79, 89
Celan, P., 117, 120
Cerquiglini, B., 128, 143
Chasseguet-Smirgel, J., 119, 143
conflict, 10, 43, 61, 103–104, 107, 113, 124, 138, 172 *see also*: Oedipal
  instinctual, 32
  intrapsychic, xxxiii, xxxv
  ongoing, 48
  unresolvable, 105
conscious(ness), xvii, 19, 119
  aspects, 112
  denial, 40
  identification, 86
  mental life, 152
  supremacy, xxxiii
  thinking, 30, 36
countertransference, xxvii, xxx, xxxvi, 13–14, 23, 40–41, 43, 47, 55, 62–63, 74, 157, 162, 164 *see also*: transference
Courtenay, M., 99
Cremerius, J., 75
Csabai, M., 177
Cyrulnik, B., 78, 89, 141, 143

Printed in Great Britain
by Amazon

70019277R00129